What others are saying—

"Thoughtful, insightful and provocative are words that best describe Chris Kulpinski's book. Our grandkids already have enough toys, gadgets and things. Why not follow Chris's very knowledgeable advice and direction and give something that will help provide our grandchildren with a financially secure future. Read, learn and enjoy the book; your grandkids will love you for it."

Richard and Adele Montgomery
Grandparents

"This book is a stimulating read that could provide the impetus and ideas to get yourself started in the investing field whether or not you have children or grandchildren. I particularly liked the references provided along with the on-line links that will give you an abundance of additional information."

John and Florence McLaughlin,
Grandparents

"Like many grandparents, we observe our grandchildren lead their lives. We see the ads that are designed to part them (and us) from their money and we see that our past is not their future. Fortunately, our grandkids are still very young, but this book has opened out eyes to what we can do to help their parents raise our grandchildren."

Ed and Patti Smith
Grandparents-in-training

"Wow! What a book. There is nothing in this book that we didn't know, but we wish someone had put all this information together earlier, so that we could have helped our kids become better managers of their money. Now we know the steps to take so that we can help our kids help our young grandchildren."

Jeff and Tina Slade
Grandparents-in training

—∿—

"I'm not a grandparent yet, as my children are just getting to the age of becoming serious about getting married and of course, I am looking forward to becoming a grandparent. It's ironic that just several months ago I was thinking how I should start planning to leave something of value to my yet unborn grandchildren. The ideas presented in this book are such a logical solution to help our children and future grandchildren improve their lives."

Cindy McLachlan
Grandparent-in-waiting

—∿—

"Like most parents, we are overwhelmed by the battle to steer a path through the peer pressure, the advertisements, the perceived needs and lack of viable role models. This book provides a way to help our kids help themselves, build self esteem and become responsible people. Why hasn't anyone thought of this simple approach earlier?"

Eric and Lisa Alinder
Parents

—∿—

It's Likely Your Grandkids Will Be Poor, Unless…

you help them reach Financial Independence

A Guide for Grandparents (and parents as well)

Chris Kulpinski

KCL
Publishing

KCL Publishing Co.,
P. O. Box 318
8711 E. Pinnacle Peak Rd.
Scottsdale, AZ 85255
www.KclPublishing.com

LCCN: 2008900187
ISBN-10 0-9814575-0-9
ISBN-13 978-0-9814575-0-9
Copyright information available upon request.

Cover Design: Manjari Graphics
Interior Design: J. L. Saloff
Graphics ©2008 istockphoto.com/Kathy Konkle
Typography: Garamond Premier Pro, Adobe Caslon Pro

v. 1.00
First Edition, 2008
Printed on acid free paper.

This book is dedicated to my grandchildren –

Jenna, Kristin and Matthew
Alex and Maisie
James and Justin

Without them being such an important part of my life,
there would be no book

If I knew grandchildren would be so much fun,
I would have had them first!

Learning to invest will hone
math skills, critical
thinking and analysis.

Table of Contents

Table of Contents

CHAPTER ONE

Introduction and Background

Your grandchildren are on their way to being poor and living poor.

A bold statement for sure, but when you step back and look at the way they're being bombarded with ads that are meant to separate them from their money, pressured by peers to conform, doted over by well-meaning parents and grandparents, who in many cases spoil them with presents rather then their presence, it appears obvious that these kids will learn too late, if ever, the true value of money.

We've all heard how our society is caught up in materialism and commercialism and consumerism. Our economy is driven by shopping. We want the latest, the biggest and the fastest. We want it now and we go into debt to get it.

It's debt we must be leery of, not materialism or consumerism, but bad debt. Bad debt is debt that costs you money; money that leaves your pocket in the form of finance payments, late charges and increased fees.

These costs, when they get out of hand, are devastating. They result in lower FICO scores, higher interest rates and lower credit.

This situation leads to a lower standard of living. It leads to living poorer.

The twenty somethings, often referred to as Generation Y or the Millennials are inheriting a world where many of the things their parents took for granted are disappearing. No more well-paying jobs, no more company provided health care and no more Social Security. Education is becoming unaffordable and low cost housing is a dream of the past.

These young adults were raised in a time of a rising stock market (1990's), grew up in an era of great wealth creation, only to watch it crumble as their elders consumed and went on a debt spending spree, as if the good times would never end.

No group of people has started life so deeply in the hole, according to a *Business Week* article; mounting college costs, dwindling financial aid, and credit card debt.

Unless our grandchildren learn some basic financial economics, they're doomed to fall into this cycle. Eventually, they may learn on their own, but by then they may already be struggling more than necessary. If they learn early in life about money, how to manage it, how to earn and invest it, they'd have a leg up in living a life that they choose.

Since this book is about creating wealth, I think it's appropriate to define the word and how I look upon the term "being wealthy".

People, of course, have their own definitions of the term, and it seems to me that the meaning changes as you become wealthier.

To those struggling to make ends meet, $100 a week more in their paycheck would make them feel wealthy. The pressure and stress of making ends meet would be reduced and would make life easier.

As you move up the income ladder, you begin to acquire more things. At first, it's a car, then eventually it's an import. At first it's a starter home, then a McMansion. It starts with a camping trip for a vacation and grows into a week or two in Mazatlan. You have the money, so you do these things.

Nothing wrong with that scene. People measure their success by the things they can buy, the things they can give their children and, in many cases, how they can outspend their friends.

All too often, the more people have, the harder they have to work to maintain and improve (whatever that might be) on what they have. They might consider themselves successful; and they are by their definition.

In a way, they, too, are living from paycheck to paycheck. If they lose their jobs, they'll be in financial trouble, just like the person struggling to make ends meet. The only difference is that these folks will be able to survive longer because they can downsize—something no one ever wants to do willingly. They'll eventually consider themselves poor, even though they may have more than a person working at a low-paying job and still struggling.

I'm sure you know or have heard of people who have little and are happy, and those who have a lot and are unhappy. The difference in this mind-set, to me, defines wealth.

Many associate wealth with money, things and what you can buy with that money.

It makes no difference how much money you have, it's what you do with it that counts. It's a mind set. It's an understanding of the value of money.

My Definition of Wealth

To me, the primary need for money is to provide a financially stressless life and by extension to provide more contentment. This allows you the freedom of having more choices. That doesn't mean that you give up the quest for more, but it does mean that you're happy with what you have, with your progress and with knowing that more is coming.

Money buys you things, but its most important function is to buy you freedom to do what you want to do. The ultimate luxury is the freedom to do what you are passionate about. You may want to get involved in various nonpaying projects and causes; you may want to explore; you may want to write or compose, or, you may want to travel at the drop of a hat. Maybe you only want to be in-

volved in short-term projects that satisfy your desires. Maybe you want to work six months a year and travel the rest of the year.

When you can do what you want, do something that gives you satisfaction and contentment, that's wealth. To achieve this goal, you need money.

The thrust of this book is to help you make apparent to your children and grandchildren the option of struggling to survive in an ever-changing world or, by your teaching them new ideas, helping them build self-confidence, analytical skills, critical thinking and trust, that they can become wealthy on their terms.

No matter how successful they become, they'll eventually have to learn how to survive that success and share it with others, but that's another story.

I would also like to point out that I'm not a financial advisor or a stockbroker. I don't write "how-to" books for a living, though

I felt compelled to write this one. I've spent my working life in the baking industry, and now I'm retired. I've had money and there were also times when there was a lack of funds.

I'm now pushing 72. I've had a good life, but looking back, I see that the evolvement of my expectations and the expansion of my perceptions has been the key to my personal wealth.

Whereas at one time I wanted more, today I want to share. I want to share information with you on how to make your grandchildren's financial lives less stressful by expanding their horizons.

There's nothing in this book that you don't know already, but it will provide you with ideas on how to share what you know with those who need to know it.

Also, you'll notice that this is a thin book. I've decided not to pad it with unnecessary fluff just to fill out the pages. I presume that you are intelligent and will understand. If you miss a point, just go back and read it again.

You and I are on the same page, otherwise you wouldn't have been attracted to this book.

All the things you want become less important once you can have anything you want.

CHAPTER TWO

A Note to Parents

These are your kids we're speaking about in this book, but we, as grandparents, have a vested interest in their well-being.

On the other hand, although this book is written primarily for grandparents, there's no reason why "grand" can't be eliminated from the words grandparent and grandchildren.

Honestly, I don't have all the answers. No one does, but with a concentrated effort and mutual understanding about what you're trying to achieve, you'll be able to contribute significantly. It's important for the kids to know their parents and grandparents are on the same page.

We elders have more time and in many cases, more disposable money to make this educational process a fun, enlightening, interesting and challenging experience for the kids.

Times are rapidly changing. To take advantage of opportunities, whether they're career-orientated or financial, our kids need to be prepared to make critical decisions that will affect their lives. It's

> ***Change is coming at us quickly, with no guide lines, no playbook and no guarantees. Be prepared.***

better to be able to recognize and evaluate choices ahead of time, not after the fact.

Informed decisions are especially important in financial matters. Life revolves around money, or whatever else is used as a medium of exchange, such as checks, credit and debit cards and even barter. Without proper understanding of money management, and in light of the rapidly changing work scene, our grandchildren, your children, will be at a disadvantage.

Just as the world and workplace has changed for you, it will more rapidly change for your children. The work force they will participate in will be far different than what you participate in, and will be completely foreign to us grandparents.

It's my intention to share with you some of my successes in this area so that you may fit them into your situation.

I hope you'll find some useful tools in the pages ahead to help you in your quest to educate your kids in financial matters. After all, this should be a family effort, but from my own experience I know that many times there are other pressing priorities.

That's why it's time for grandparents to step up to the plate and help you make their grandchildren financially savvy and therefore financially independent.

CHAPTER THREE

A Note to Grandparents

This book is written for grandparents, by a grandparent. We're not trying to usurp the authority of the parents, but we know that in today's changing work environment many families have both parents working.

Everyday concerns must take precedence, and sometimes the future is left to the future. That's not a situation I personally relish. I want to be active in creating my future experiences, rather than let them just happen without my input.

I'm sure that from your vantage point, and with your experience, you agree it's better to be in control of what's going to happen to you rather than letting it evolve through happenstance.

To control your own shots, you need an expanded view of what's possible, you need skills that are neglected in our educational system and you need to be financially savvy.

These are the things I will be expanding on in this book, and specifically, what you can do, along with the parents, to educate your grandchildren to meet the rapidly advancing future in a confident manner.

Some who have previewed this work say it is a wake-up call for grandparents, a call to arms to help guide their grandkids in a very uncertain future.

Some parents might view this as interference in the lives of their children. Some parents might feel this is an intrusion into their lives. Some grandparents might feel this is overstepping their relationship with their kids and grandkids.

That's not the case. This exercise is to be undertaken with the advice, consent and the participation of the parents.

I'm suggesting that you take the lead in this educational process, and I spell out steps to help you make this a reality.

> ***We alone are responsible for our successes. Let teaching our grandchildren about financial independence be one of these successes.***

CHAPTER FOUR

The Future

"*Everyone needs to think differently about the future, a future that is riddled with change, challenge and risk. It is a new kind of future, not the steady plodding of progress from one moment to the next, punctuated by brief bursts of progress from one moment to the next, punctuated by brief bursts of innovation that characterizes much of history. Now we face a post 9/11 future. The future of our lives, of our work, of our businesses—and most of all the future of our world—depend on us gaining new understanding of the dizzying changes that lie ahead.*"[1]

That is a profound statement.

---

1. Excerpt from James Canton's "The Extreme Future: The Top: Trends That Will Reshape the World in the Next 5,10 and 20 Years"

Change is coming at an accelerated pace. A convergence of different disciplines, from globalization to technological advances to an energy crisis and climate change, is already forcing all of us to become aware of the rapid march into the future.

Changes that are the result of planned research and development, and changes that are beyond our control, are happening at this very moment.

Many choose to ignore it, many feel that technology will save us, while others are trying to make the rest of us at least aware that we'll have to make drastic changes in the future. We need to be aware of the advancing changes and try to plan for them.

We've not yet begun to realize the full impact of globalization, technology and innovation on our future lives. To be able to financially navigate through this morass, we must educate our grandchildren to be discerning adults, fully in charge of their own finances while mastering their conflicting needs and wants.

Whereas at one time we had the luxury of time to make decisions and plans, we are now entering a period of change so rapid and ongoing that we need to be prepared in advance for any eventuality.

To live in the future we have to plan for the future.

You may think that you don't know what the future will hold, but I maintain that you do. It's just that most of us don't know how to react or plan for it.

James Canton, in his book *The Extreme Future*, speaks of a

future that is full of scientific advances that will allow us to live longer and more productive lives, a life where robots will do much of the mundane work, where nanotechnology will help create solutions to many of our problems, including aging and energy.

One caveat to this scenario is that America is not well-positioned to spearhead this thrust because of the inadequacies in our educational system. Other countries are now producing the mathematicians and scientists. Many of these foreign students learn at American universities, which decry the lack of qualified or interested American students coming into these important fields.

Because of outsourcing, old industrial-age jobs are disappearing. And unless we prepare for the convergence of the Information Age and the Innovation Age, those new jobs centered around technology and innovation will also be outsourced.

Another and I feel more eminent future problem is our looming energy crisis. It's not a matter of if, but when, and I believe the when is sooner than later.

We're all aware that oil production has peaked; new discoveries of oil can not replace the present demand, much less the growing demand. America is using more oil, and the growth in demand from China, India and other developing countries is voracious.

Alternative energies, such as wind and solar power, will not drive transportation. The use of hydrogen is not viable in the near future. Corn-produced ethanol is not economical and only replaces about 15% of gasoline. Meanwhile, the cost of food-stuffs dependent on corn rises.

Even if we quadrupled our solar and wind capacity (which isn't likely) that wouldn't replace oil, gas or coal in the production of electricity. It takes a decade to build a nuclear plant.

As more countries demand more energy and wars break out over the control of what oil there is, what do think will happen when the price of gasoline is $10 or more per gallon?

Obviously, the price of everything will increase rapidly. Income will not rise, because there will be no increase in productivity, only in the cost of materials. This will lead to inflation, and possible hyper-inflation. The Federal Reserve can print more money and subsidize everyone, but that's not a likely policy.

The point is, whatever the future, will our grandchildren be prepared to face these challenges, both from an educational and financial position?

Our grandchildren are not aware of many of these impending changes, just as we weren't aware that our lives would be completely disrupted by globalization, new technology and dazzling innovations. When we grandparents were teenagers, we weren't aware that computers, cell phones, space travel, different medical advances, quantum physics or oil shortages were around the corner. As fast as these changes came upon us, the changes in the future will come even more rapidly and will include disruptive changes in retirement and medical benefits.

Although there might be isolated bright spots, our educational system is not teaching our grandkids the skills they need to deal with and prosper within the changes that lie ahead.

Our schools, primary, high school and even college, teach skills needed to survive in an Industrial Age, not in the Age of Technology and Innovation.

Our schools are not instilling within our students the excitement of science, math and analytical thinking.

Kids primarily do things they're good at because it's fun for them, because those interests are exciting and challenging.

Science and math are challenging, but they're not fun because our school systems, on the whole, haven't made them interesting.

Schools aren't the only institutions not meeting these challenges. Our politicians are also at fault. They can't agree on a policy to set a direction, so they do nothing.

Why this inertia from both schools and government? Because both are averse to change. They have a vested interest in keeping things status quo. And special interests that also have a vested interest in keeping the status quo.

It's easier to maintain the status quo than to fight for change, and if someone proposes change and fails, well, there is always Plan B—the status quo.

An example is the need for changes in Medicare and Social Security. There has been talk for years of the need to adopt changes, but that's all there is—talk.

There was talk, during the 2007 presidential debates, of personalizing Social Security and Medicare and mandating health insurance. Some espouse a one-payer plan i.e., the government is the provider. Others propose a self-directed plan. And, of course, there's always the status quo if we can't reach consensus! We're arguing and can't agree on what's best for us.

Whatever happens, or whenever these changes occur, and they will have to occur, will our grandchildren be prepared to financially cope with the changes?

One way or another, the cost of any social security or health program will still be borne by the individual, either through taxation or the private purchase of health insurance and contributions toward a pension account.

Will our grandkids be in a financial position to easily cope with these new demands? They'll have to cope, but wouldn't it be better if they were knowledgeable about their options?

Think about this—a million dollars in net worth really isn't enough to allow a retirement that will allow you to do the things you might like to do. This dollar figure will only go up in the future. Will our grandkids be prepared?

Your grandchildren need your presence more than your presents.

Are You Ready for...

- Living and working in a virtual world?
- The birthright of living over a hundred years?
- Vast identity theft through technology?
- Chip implants for better information about you?
- Having yourself cloned?
- Enhancement drugs?
- Gene manipulation?
- Not aging?
- Ingesting bacteria to help improve your immune system?
- Replacing all parts of your body with your own cells?
- Personal robotics?
- Using asphalt on your roof as a solar panel?
- Faster everything?

There's no mystery or uncertainty that there are other vast changes coming.

- We'll need to find substitute energy sources.

- The climate is changing; eventually it will disrupt weather patterns, which in turn will slowly alter agriculture, precipitation and where people will live.

- The population of the world is rapidly expanding, putting a strain on our resources.

- Changes are coming because of technological advancements.

Whenever civilizations moved from one age to another, there were great disruptions. Many people couldn't adapt and were left behind.

We went from being hunter-gatherers, to becoming an Agricultural Society, to an Industrial Society, to an Information Society and now we're entering the Innovation Age.

The time-span between ages is getting shorter and shorter, and it has become more difficult for many people to adapt. We were hunter-gatherers for tens of thousands of years, an Agrarian Society for thousands of years, an Industrial society for only several hundred years, Information years, just a few decades. The Information and Innovation Ages are merging and eventually will become something else.

People of course adapt but many do not, especially in transitional periods such as we are in now. Studies show that 67% of the baby boomers don't have enough money saved for retirement. Many current seniors are struggling.

As you are well aware, parenting is a full-time occupation but, because of the rapid changes in the last decade, most households have both parents working.

Today, parents are overwhelmed with work, responsibilities to their children and the need for some downtime for themselves.

This is where it's time for grandparents to step forward and help fill the gap. We need to make our grandchildren aware of impending changes, and we need to educate them to become financially independent so that they'll be in the position to make choices.

Our decisions today as grandparents will impact our grandchildrens' futures and the decisions that they will have to make. Will their decision patterns be focused around surviving, or will they be able to make choices that allow them to live a life that is financially stress-free?

We have to anticipate and participate in creating our future; otherwise, it will come upon us without our consent. From our life's experiences, we know that to be a fact, but our grandchildren do not. Wouldn't it be better if they were in a position to create the future they want because you took the time to mentor them?

Our grandchildren need a vision of the possibilities. You, as a grandparent, have to help otherwise, your grandchildren might be among those left behind because of impending changes.

*Signs that Point to the Future**

- What does it mean for the future of entertainment if 80 percent of consumers are on the Internet downloading games, video, music, and information?

- What does it mean for the future of health care if 90 percent of consumers want tests to reveal their genetic destiny?

- How will online sales be hurt in the future if identity theft continues and better security doesn't emerge?

- What does it mean for industry and society if one hundred million consumers control $20 trillion of assets and want to live to age one hundred as healthy and active as they can be?

- What does it mean to the workforce if we do not attract 20 million immigrants into the U.S. within fifteen years?

- What does it mean to China if that country continues to grow without becoming a democracy?

- What does it mean to global peace and security if terrorists, drug dealers, and organized crime link up to attack the world's institutions?

- What does it mean to Africa and the world if we do not work to cure AIDS and stop emerging pandemics?

- What does it mean to global growth and productivity if we do not discover new energy sources as oil supplies are dwindling?

- What is the future of society if global warming and climate change are not resolved by 2050, when there will be close to nine billion people on the planet?

* The Extreme Future; James Canton

CHAPTER FIVE

What's Out There Now

There are many books and tons of information on the Internet about money, getting a job, the necessity of saving, the stock market, but nothing really about teaching your children and grandchildren how to be financially independent—how to be an investor while making your own decisions.

There's much said and written about the importance of investing, but it's all predicated on your allowing someone else make the decisions for you.

There are hundreds of sites on the Internet where you can find people talking about stock picks. There are more than you want to know about. The majority don't teach you how to create a strategy to invest for yourself.

One of the best offerings is the KidsWealth Money Management Program (www.KidsWealth.com.) offered by KidsWealth (USA), Inc. This program teaches children between the ages of 4 to 12 how to manage real money and make real money choices / decisions.

The simplicity and beauty of the KidsWealth Money Management Program is that it is easily integrated into any family lifestyle and value/belief system. It can also be utilized within any economic structure across the globe (because money is money no matter where you live).

Just as kids need training wheels when first learning to ride a bicycle, think of KidsWealth as the training wheels to teach your grandkids a *balanced* approach to money management.

Once kids start to learn how to manage their money and watch their wealth grow, they will then be ready to understand how to utilize their wealth to make more wealth through different avenues such as investing.

Technology is neat, but it doesn't solve the basic problem. If most of the pros have a difficult time beating the market, what makes you think that some anonymous poster on a blog has the answers?

Investing is a long term strategy; it's not about stock picking. Yes, if you're in the stock market, you have to pick some stocks, but it should be with an eye to the long term, unless you want to become a day trader.

To be an investor you have to have a different mind-set than most people grow up with. From the very start we're taught to listen and obey, to follow the rules and get a job, to save some money for a vacation or other necessities. You're encouraged to save your money in an interest-bearing account or, if you want a piece of the American dream, invest it in a mutual fund. Buy a home. Want to get adventurous? Start investing in individual stocks or even start a business.

Many people became rich investing that way. Others failed miserably along the way. Why did some fail and others succeed?

People succeed or fail because they're either prepared or not prepared. They don't do well in the stock market because they don't take time to learn about *how to decide* on a particular mutual fund or stock. They might follow the advice of a guru, investment reports or their own stock brokers.

Remember, these advisors are employees of a financial institution, and they're paid to promote the products of their employer. They advise you to purchase what will make their company money, not necessarily what will truly benefit you. They're handicapped by being able to provide you with their employer's product only. It doesn't mean that these products are bad, but they may not be right for you. There could be other options the advisor might not be aware of, or if he is, he can't suggest them to you.

Don't misunderstand, as individuals, they may care about your well-being, but as employees they may be prevented from helping you maximize your returns.

Have you noticed how all the investment ads on TV have a disclaimer about what they just advertised?

Dealing with these institutions isn't always wrong, but the decisions of how and where to invest should be made with due diligence on your part. It's your money; take care of it.

If you choose to use an advisor, use one that doesn't sell any product, but is well-versed in the majority of choices. He makes his money by advising you, not by selling you a product.

Also, to be fair, there are some financial advisors that will recommend product that is not sold or available from the company they represent.

People become self-employed in their quest for financial freedom. Many people have become rich by having their own business, others are barely eking out a living, and even more have closed their doors. Why did some fail and others succeed?

People struggle or fail at being self-employed because they lack the mind set of someone who's determined to make their dream a reality. They don't do the due diligence to help them decide on the right course of action, and many times there is no Plan B.

People start a business because they want to be their own boss. They take their specific skills (electrician, carpenter, etc) and strike out on their own. They don't realize that there are three roles an entrepreneur has to perform. He or she has to be visionary (where do your want your business to go), you have to be able to manage your business on a daily basis (find new customers, pay the bills, etc), and you have to perform the functions of that business (i.e., using that skill you possess to get paid).

After all, most start out as a one-person shop. It's difficult being all three when you're busy performing the daily tasks of doing business. These people have essentially "purchased their job". They're their own boss, but they're probably working harder than ever. Many fail.

The mind-set of a true entrepreneur or an investor is different from that of an employee or self-employed individual. An investor or entrepreneur is mentally prepared to take the steps needed to succeed, to act; whereas the employee may think about the possibilities, but not always act on them. They don't take steps to find out what it takes to get out of the rat race because they're too busy being in the rat race.

It's important to recognize that even business owners and investors fail.

It's not the scope of this book to venture into the area of why; just remember, not everyone is successful in every venture.

In school you learn how to be on time, be a team player and follow directions. These are important traits; however, there are no classes for youngsters on how to think like an entrepreneur or an investor, no classes on how to take charge of financial dreams, no classes on being a critical and analytical thinker.

And, since money and finances are usually not discussed around the dinner table, our children and grandchildren are not exposed to these topics at home.

What to Do With What's Out There

No one knows everything. Once you realize you don't know something and you want to find out, you have to know where to look for answers.

I've found that the easiest way to get answers is to ask someone who's doing what you want answers about. You'd be surprised how willing people are to share information on their area of expertise.

Schools have a role in teaching some financial literacy, and yet kids get most of their information from their parents and grandparents. On the other hand, many parents don't discuss financial matters with their kids because they feel the children are too young; or they shouldn't be concerned about such matters; in fact, the parents may not feel competent in discussing such a topic.

But remember, whatever you know is more than your child knows. So start. Don't worry, they don't have to know how the Federal Reserve sets monetary policy, nor do they care. Kids should be fed information in an age-sensitive manner. The older they are, the more complex the information.

Even simple lessons are very important. I just read an article stating that in 2006, 180,000 young adults between the ages of 18 and 25 declared bankruptcy. If that doesn't motivate you to help your grandkids change their thinking, then I don't know what will.

There are all types of seminars for adults on how they should invest their money—usually with someone else. Those people want

> ***We give them money, but in many cases, see it spent frivolously. We marvel at their technical skills, yet wonder if they need the latest gadget.***

you to let them make your decisions for you. After all, they're the experts. That may be fine for some, but wouldn't it be better if you never had to attend one of those seminars on how to make millions? Wouldn't it have been great if someone had mentored you when you were a youngster in how to achieve financial independence on you own so that you could be in control of the direction of your future?

I'm not suggesting that you avoid all these seminars. I find many of them to be a great source of new ideas.

There are also financial boot camps for rich kids where they learn macroeconomics, spend their checks and "win" if there's any money left over. These educational camps are underwritten in many cases by banks and credit card companies. Does that tell you anything? Credit cards are about debt. It's nice to save pennies, but you should really be concentrating on making dollars.

And of course there's the Internet. There's a lot of information, but you have to be selective. In the resource section at the end of the book, I've listed a number of websites that are unbiased, share information and ideas and are excellent teaching tools for expanding your base of knowledge. Remember, they're only tools for you to use and take advantage of and should not be the only source of decision making.

You earn money when you work for it; you make money when it comes to you as passive income, money that you don't have to work for. That's what investing is all about, and that's what you want to teach your grandkids.

If what you think is true about your money isn't, when would you want to know? Stockbrokers tell you that the only safe and prudent investing strategy is diversification. Depending on your age, a certain percent should be in stocks and the balance in bonds. They tell you that risk is dangerous and should, under most circumstance, be avoided.

That's not necessarily the case today. With globalization, worldwide money markets, a growing world economy, rapid and often instant worldwide financial transaction and easy access to knowledge, your grandchildren will need to know how to manage their own portfolio, and how to make their own informed financial decisions. Managing and controlling risk is one of these skills.

Do you realize how much money various intermediaries take out of your nest egg? Do you realize that the government can't wait for you to draw down your IRA so they can start taxing it? Do you realize that our dollars are only supported by the good will of, and in, our government? Wouldn't it be better if you were able

Are You Ready for...

- You can't learn to play music just by learning to read notes, you have to play an instrument

- You can't learn to play ball just by reading the rules, you have to play the game.

- You can't learn to read by learning the alphabet, you have to read words.

- You can't learn to fly an airplane by studying aerodynamics, you have to get into the cockpit.

- You can't learn to be financially independent by keeping your money in the bank, you have to learn to invest it.

to analyze and critically review your options before you made your investment?

So what can you do? How can you make your children and grandchildren think like investors, to think as owners of their own businesses, want to take charge of their financial independence?

You become a investing mentor and you let them participate in the decision making process. You let them see the results of their decisions, good or bad, and you let them enjoy the fruits of their labors.

You have to become the mentor, the teacher, the guiding light. How, you ask? Read on.

> *Knowledge is power and knowledge comes from information.*

CHAPTER SIX

Why You Should Help Your Grandchildren Become Financially Savvy

As the commercial pointed out—"This is not your father's Oldsmobile".

The world is changing and it's changing fast. Today's jobs are becoming as antiquated as that of the horse-drawn buggy builder and the jobs that no longer produce the Oldsmobile.

Technology and innovation are changing everything: the careers that will be available, the skills that will be needed, lifestyle flexibility, adaptation to new social demands and expectations. To survive and adapt to the changes, a well-grounded financial education is very important.

Today, it's imperative that we explain to our children and grandchildren that the days of job security are over. Employer paid health insurance is finished. Medicare is facing huge deficits. Social Security is facing diminishing contributions at a time when payments and retirees are increasing. There will have to be changes to these government sponsored benefits.

The political scene is littered with suggestions to change these institutions. We and our politicians have known of these looming problems for a decade at least, but there's no agreement as to what is "best". Between vested interests, an entrenched bureaucracy, the desire to be reelected and a complacent electorate, finding the solution is being passed on to future generations.

Even old-fashioned employer sponsored, "guaranteed" pensions are in doubt, as are union sponsored plans. Many companies fail and their obligations are passed on to the Pension Benefit Guaranty Corporation which is an independent agency of the United States government. The agency was created by the Employee Retirement Income Security Act of 1974 (ERISA) to protect the pensions of employees of failed companies.

Wouldn't it be great if none of these problems would affect your grandchildren? Wouldn't it be great if they had the financial savvy to be financially independent and therefore not adversely affected by any third-party decision concerning pensions, Social Security or health insurance?

Our grandchildren will be responsible for their entire financial well-being for the rest of their lives. Over time, there will be no more guarantees. That's why financial intelligence is vital. It gives them choices and control over their lives.

Living paycheck to paycheck will not be an option. There will be no guarantee of a paycheck, or a pension, or of health insurance. They'll have to provide for themselves. We're in a disruptive change, a change from an Industrial Age to an Information and

Innovation Age. Many of us have already been ensnared in these changes.

A convergence of various disciplines from globalization and technological changes to climate change and an energy crisis will create huge opportunities and, just as equally, huge threats to our way of life unless we're prepared to deal with them.

Even now, many people are caught up in these changes and are wondering what's happening. They did all the things they were told to do, i.e. go to school, study hard, get a job, save some money, buy a home, then retire and enjoy the "good life".

However, that's not what's happening to many people. They don't see the light at the end of the tunnel. Many of us live paycheck to paycheck, have more than one job and, as is the norm today, the spouse is also working.

Some mornings you lie in bed and wonder why. Why am I struggling, why don't I have the job I studied for, why am I working so hard and have very little to show for it? What am I going to do if my company downsizes, my job is exported abroad or my company fails? Why am I in this dead-end job, in fact I'm beginning to hate this job because it is so mundane and repetitious.

In fact, for many people, their life becomes their job. They work just to survive. They work to make a buck, and they work and they work and they work. Do we really want this for our grandchildren?

Many people have jobs that don't pay enough for them to

make ends meet. Many have two jobs. They did everything right but life didn't work out for them. They could probably give you a dozen reasons why but can't stop to talk because they have to make that buck. They feel life hasn't been fair to them, and they struggle and struggle and struggle with no end in sight.

These are the people with poor credit, so they can't purchase a house, they pay high interest on their credit cards, carry large debts and might even use the paycheck cashing establishment down the street for short term loans for which they pay exorbitant rates. They can't seem to dig themselves out of the hole. Do we really want this for our grandchildren?

As I write this (2007), our country is in the throes of a sub-prime mortgage meltdown. At the moment, there's no end in sight. Many people have lost, or are on the verge, of losing their homes. Seminars are popping up telling you how to get rich on these home foreclosures.

What happened? There are numerous reasons and much finger pointing, but the primary reason, in my opinion, is that many people wanted to enhance their financial positions. Can't fault them for that, but they can be faulted for not doing any critical and analytical due diligence. Like many, they felt that whatever happened today will continue to happen tomorrow. If prices are going up today, they'll continue to go up tomorrow.

The financial press and evening news played up the real estate phenomenon. Reasons were given why this growth will continue and why everyone should join the rush.

Many of you remember the old adage, "When your shoeshine boy talks of the stocks he owns, it's time to get out." When the talk around the office water cooler is about the stocks you own, it is time to consider getting out, not getting in. When you overhear the person making your latte telling his coworkers of the condo or spec home they just purchased for speculation, it's time to get out.

These sudden extended spurts of growth create bubbles which must eventually burst. Rather than following the herd mentality, critical analysis is called for, some due diligence is warranted, forward looking thinking is demanded.

Where do you learn this stuff? Well, financial education never stops, but it must first begin, sooner rather than later.

As our grandkids learn about making money, they'll become enthused because it's like a game. In a game, you know the rules, you know how to play and you automatically react to any circumstances. This is true on the ball field or on a computer game. Make the wrong decisions, you lose.

When you first start to play, you make a lot of errors, but the longer you play the better you get, the better you understand the game and the better your chance of winning as you improve your skills.

And so it is in real life and, in this case with real money. Errors early in the financial game are less costly than errors made later in life. The sooner you learn to play the game, the better.

Understanding and winning at the financial game will allow our grandchildren to control their lives. Knowledge is power and power is the ability to do what you want.

With financial knowledge, your grandchild can pursue his own passion, be an entrepreneur, travel, further their education and help propel their own kids into the future.

Financial knowledge and therefore financial independence will allow them to adapt faster, innovate smarter and prepare them for the changes facing them. This financial knowledge will allow them to concentrate on their lives rather than on making ends meet.

And all this because you helped them get started.

The Value of Debt

Bad Debt

There's bad debit, and there's good debt. Simply put, bad debt costs you money, good debt makes you money.

Bad debit is credit card debt that isn't paid in full monthly. If you're only paying the minimum, the credit card company loves you as a customer.

Bad debt is any debt that is incurred when you purchase something you can not pay for immediately, or at the end of a normal billing cycle. It takes a lot of money to buy the things you may not need.

There may be times when you have to resort to this type of debt, but if you do, make sure the debt is paid off as quickly as possible. Use this type of debt VERY sparingly. If you can't pay for it, think twice about purchasing it.

You pay this debt by working and using funds from your paycheck, funds that could go into savings and investments.

The Wall Street Journal reported that 1% of the wealthiest people earned 21.2% of all the income in 2005. Forbes mentions, "The collective net worth of the nation's mightiest plutocrats rose from $290 billion to 1.5 trillion", which means that the *Forbes* 400 own more than 13% of the gross national product of the United States.

On the other hand, according to *The Wall Street Journal*, 50% of the bottom earners earned only 12.8% of the gross national product.

How do these low earners manage? By using credit and incurring debt. We live by credit. We buy our homes on credit, our furniture on credit, the food we eat on credit, our vacation on credit and even the latte on credit.

When I was a kid, cash was king. When I became an adult, credit became king. Now not only grown-ups, but teenagers are flashing their credit cards.

If you can't pay the entire amount on the credit card, you have the potential to get yourself mired in a downward spiral of consumer debt, finance charges and low credit scores. This leads to making it more difficult to get credit when needed, such as purchasing a home or a car, which leads to higher interest rates, higher charges and bigger debt.

As your debt grows, your choices become limited. Your struggle becomes more difficult and debt breeds more debt. You become a prisoner of your own debt.

This is bad debt.

Credit cards are neither good nor bad, but they can kill you financially and ruin your life.

Good Debt

Good debt, on the other hand, is debt paid with someone else's money.

An example would be if you take out a home equity loan, purchase a rental property and have both your home equity loan and mortgage on the rental property repaid by the rent collected monthly.

In this scenario, you gain by having a property that's paying off your loan, providing you with a positive cash flow and appreciating in value over the years.

You have to teach your grandchildren this understanding of debt. If the debt is paid off through an investment and its repayment is not coming out of your earnings from your line of work, then that's good debt.

Learning to use credit and learning to avoid bad debt are key to helping your grandchildren become financially savvy, financially successful and financially independent. Without this basic information, they could become mired in a life of swimming upstream just to exist.

Learning early on in life to preserve money is key. This discipline will allow you to become financially secure as you build your investing nest egg.

Even investing small amounts of money on a steady and consistent basis will yield large returns in the long run. It's better to start systematic saving early. The difference in returns due to compounded interest is huge.

That's one reason I started an investment club with my grandkids; to teach them that small amounts of money can grow to be sizable sums. To this day, they still operate the investment club, even while working to get their graduation gift and, in Alex's case, to make that gift grow. (See Chapter 8)

Recently, I heard on TV that more and more college students

are turning to private sources of funding as tuitions go up and government support is reduced. These private loans are at high percentage rates and many graduates will find themselves with huge debt when they graduate, and entering the work force. How will they dig themselves out of the hole? Although they received an education, this is still bad debt. Maybe they wouldn't find themselves in that position if they had received some earlier help in becoming financially savvy.

On the other hand, many people work because they want the nice things: a large home, a luxurious car, an extravagant vacation. They want to live rich because they want to feel rich. As Robert T. Kiyosaki, author of the *Rich Dad, Poor Dad* series of books, points out, they want the "doodads". They want the material things that make them feel good. They feel good by having these items, showing these items to others and mingling with people who have the same doodads. These folks make a lot of money, but that doesn't allow them to slow down; they have to make money to pay for the things that make them feel good. It's expensive to buy the things they don't need. They're in a rat race, can't slow down and don't know how to get out.

I have several rental properties. Some of the rent is subsidized by the federal government. I have no problem with that, but I have a problem with the fact that the poorest families have huge plasma TVs, the latest electronic equipment and, although the cars are not BMW's or a Benz, they are fairly expensive and new.

These people will always be renters, and very likely be subsidized. Unfortunately, these families have never been taught the value of money. In preparing for this book, I asked two of my renters what they would do if they suddenly found themselves with an extra $5,000.

One said that she would buy things for the house, give her daughter money to buy new clothes and spend the rest on herself. I asked her if these were purchases that she would NOT have considered if she did not have the money. She said she only considered these choices because the $5,000 was newfound money.

The other said she would buy a new car, even though there was nothing wrong with the car she had. She just wanted a newer car.

Neither said that they would pay off debt or put the money into savings.

Because most of us work so hard, we have little time left for the things we really want to do i.e. to enjoy what we have, to enjoy our families and friends, and live an unhurried and uncluttered life. Sure, we get our vacations, but how many of us would give our right arm to go in to work at a later time, leave earlier to attend our child's or grandchild's ball game or recital, or just take some extra time off without it affecting our finances?

Wouldn't you really prefer to take a trip rather than a vacation? People who have the time, take a trip. They go wherever and whenever they wish.

A vacation is taken by those who have limited time and are usually told by their employer when they can use that time.

The Value of Money

How do we explain to the kids that we love them but we can't—can't go to the recital, can't go to the ball game, can't take them to the movies, can't go bike riding with them or take them to the zoo? We know that we should be spending time with them. We know they need and want our personal attention and approval but we don't have time to spend with them because we're too busy making money to buy them, and ourselves the things we think we/they want and need.

We soothe our guilt by buying them "stuff" to show that we love them. Love is, in many cases, displayed through material things. Eventually, it becomes the accepted norm. Think about it. Does it show the child how much you love them, or does it mask your guilt? Do you buy it because it's needed, or because it's wanted? Do you buy it because it's easier than telling your child or grandchild no.

In addition, peer pressure can be an insidious thing. It's difficult to deal with, and in many cases kids go with the flow. The want becomes a need "because everyone else has one".

Learning the value of money and, just as importantly, how

to make it, goes a long way toward helping your child make wiser financial decisions.

Studies show that many grandparents are concerned about their grandchildren knowing the value of money, and large percentages are afraid that giving the kids too much will spoil them. They're also concerned, because they, themselves, may be financially strapped and are afraid that their grandchildren might find themselves in that position.

Stories are appearing in the press about credit cards being given to kids entering college, and in some cases, while they are still in high school. Has anyone taught these youngsters about debt?

I have become aware that many college graduates who are seeking well paying jobs in various corporations are being turned down because of bad credit rating.

You read that right; a bad credit rating, a low FICO score. Students are graduating with large credit card debt, reflecting poor money management skills. A college education isn't much good without a financial education.

The key word is management. If you can't manage your own resources, how can we expect you to manage ours?

Our grandchildren are bombarded by ads depicting the latest trends, the latest gadgets, the latest styles. Most of these ads feature starlets, sport stars or "look alikes," whose only job is to separate our kids from their money.

Why You Need to Motivate Your Grandkids

- There will be no job, health or pension guarantees in the future.

- The tools our grandchildren need to achieve financial success are not taught in school.

- The information provided by the media, stockbrokers, and get-rich-quick deals is often misleading and biased. You'd better know how to separate the wheat from the chaff.

- Who will teach them the value of money if not you and their parents?

- There's good debt and there is bad debt and it's important to know the difference as early in life as possible.

- Knowledge is power.

In many cases, these celebrity figures, who often end up in rehab or jail, are portrayed as, or become role models for your grandchildren.

There's a better way for the kids to get anything they want, for you to spend a lot of quality time with them, and for everyone to have the life they always wanted. In the process, you'll teach them how to become financially self-reliant.

Why should you do this? Simple. They're your grandchildren and you love them. They sure are more fun than your kids were at this age, don't you think?

Expansion of Our Awareness

As our civilization progresses, new sciences, discoveries and inventions not only make our life easier, but help us understand things about ourselves and our universe.

I've just read a review of a book[1] in which the author puts forth the proposition that all inventions and discoveries of the past have been accomplished because that particular individual was able to take different pieces of information that were already available and put them together to create the new discovery or invention. The divergent ideas were already in place, they just needed someone to bring them together. People who are successes at anything got

---

1 "Smart World; Breakthrough Creativity and the New Science of Ideas," by Richard Ogle, Harvard Business School Press

there, because they were able to bring together various resources to help them succeed.

In the past, because communications were slow it took a long time for ideas to suddenly become a new invention or discovery. Today, our ever increasing advancements are the results of collaboration and rapid communication.

I tend to agree with that observation. Everyone has the talent, but to use it you have to have an open mind and be receptive to, and look for, new ideas. And, to connect the dots, you have to be aware and persistent.

That's one of the premises of this book. Our grandchildren need to have their horizons expanded while they're young. When they get to be older, they, as did most of us, become entrenched in what is familiar and comfortable. They need to be comfortable with change. If they're to be financially independent, they have to be on that mental track from an early age.

Financial success opens doors to many possibilities and opportunities. Financial independence allows choice.

Are You Ready For...

I'm sure that you heard or read that the United States is too materialistic, too consumer spending orientated, that we need to save more and spend less. There's proposal that instead of an income tax, there should be a flat sales tax, where you pay up to 25% tax on every purchase that you make. If that won't make people think twice about buying "doo-dads" and "stuff", I don't know what will.

But, if such a proposal would pass Congress, do you realize what it will do to our economy? There would a drastic slowdown because our GNP is driven by consumer spending. What would THAT do your grandchild's job or career?

There are no easy answers, but it's time they learn how to invest so that they can easily, and without stress, survive such changes.

CHAPTER SEVEN

Why People Fall Into Financial Traps

My parents didn't teach me about finances. I was expected to go to school, study hard, get a job and pay my bills. We didn't have credit cards, cash was still acceptable and, in many cases, the only way to pay your everyday bills. My parents would go to the local electric company store to pay the electric bills. We had no telephone.

There were banks for businesses and savings and loan offices for the worker.

My father went to the savings and loan office to pay our mortgage and, you were allowed to run up a tab at your local grocers until payday. That, in many cases, was the extent of your debt—the grocer.

Only businesses used checks. You got paid by check and usually cashed it at the grocer's and paid him any monies owed. The milkman and the bread delivery driver got paid weekly, or whenever you were at home.

I didn't teach my kids very much about finance either, other than some basics. They learned about checking and savings accounts and my wife showed them how to balance a checkbook. We told them they had to go to school, study hard and get a good job. It would be nice, we said, if they could get a job that would allow them to do what they like, but don't count on it.

However, they very likely would have a job for life, a pension, either from the company or union, a health care plan, and Social Security with Medicare from the government. If they were frugal, some savings would make their old age easier. I didn't tell them about the stock market, mortgages or debt. These were just part of everyday life that you learned as time went on.

As a kid, my only exposure to the stock market was when my Dad told me that my grandfather invested in the stock of City Service, an oil company that today is known as Citgo. It was our family's first venture into stocks (late 1940s) and I thought (I was about 12) it was neat that we owned a part of an oil company. I never heard any more about it until one day I overheard the adults speaking of how risky the stock market was, and it was only for the moneyed class. I didn't understand at the time, but later I realized that my grandfather had lost on the stock. To my knowledge, my grandfather never purchased stock again, and my father started possibly in his 60s. Any wonder why I didn't know anything about stocks?

Nor were there such things as credit cards. Today, credit cards are as ubiquitous as cell phones. Even youngsters are encouraged by credit card companies to use credit cards. The only problem is that as credit card companies encourage our kids to spend, very few kids are making the payments. Their parents are—with their own money. How can kids learn financial management from that?

Plastic doesn't represent real money. Plastic is a form of bad debt with stiff penalty charges if used incorrectly.

The schools my kids attended, like most schools, taught them how to read, write and do some math and a few other things. They taught them everything they needed to know about entering the work force to make their way through life—punctuality (be there when the school bell rings), fulfilling assignments (doing your homework), teamwork (sports, band, choir, etc)—all the things that are expected of you in the mass production workplace they were about to enter. These are important traits; however, at some point in your life you have to become independent and think for yourself.

The kids weren't taught critical thinking or decision making or analysis. Even today, many corporate recruiters complain that college graduates don't have these critical skills. Yes, they read and, in some cases, even write cohesive reports, but can they analyze, can they take opposing views and data and make a critical decision?

So it shouldn't be surprising that so many people have the wrong idea of what it means to be financially secure. Does it mean having a well-paying job or career? Does it mean having your own home and a fancy car? Does it mean that Social Security and Medicare will take care of us in our older years? Does it mean that maybe the stock market will always do better in the future and you'll have some extra funds?

Maybe, but certainly that won't be the scenario for our grandchildren. There will be some form of Social Security and health insurance. The public will demand that of its government. But who will the government tax to raise the funds to pay for this as our work force gets smaller?

No one told the kids of previous generations that the world was changing therefore many adults do not recognize the tremendous chances that are occurring. Oh, we all see the incremental changes and we shake our heads in disbelief, but we go on with our lives. I've made it this far so I'm okay, we say to ourselves. Meanwhile, what we were taught and what is relevant in today's world are miles apart.

Except for one thing—schools still teach the same stuff and no one teaches our kids how to avoid the rat race that most of us are trapped in. Basic economics aren't taught, and our schools still aren't teaching critical thinking or decision making or analysis.

Why are our lives in financial peril? Because no one gave us any guidance as to how to become financially self-sufficient. That includes our parents as well as our schools. Guidance provided by stockbrokers, financial advisors and banks is self-serving.

Meanwhile, all these changes that have been going on behind our backs are now squarely in our faces. We now have to take responsibility for our own finances—but we were never shown how. And the changes will only come faster.

From having job security, health security and old-age security, we're suddenly made to realize that's no longer the case. We'll have some of those benefits, but not enough. We haven't saved enough for our retirements, and many of us don't know where to begin.

Kids are very keen observers and their natural assumption is that what they see around them is the accepted norm. They emulate their parents and are influenced by their surroundings.

They're exposed to commercials, celebrity and entertainment hype, ads for the latest must have trendy doodads. They observe how people, including their family, live by watching various TV programs and movies, and they make judgments. In many cases the judgment is "I want that," or "I want to be like that," because that's the way it is and I should have that.

Many of us fall prey to the commercials, the hype and the

glamorization of unrealistic expectations. Just as most of our kids are doing today, we were mesmerized by the glamour of the movies, TV, sport stars and celebrities. We wanted what we saw on TV and in the movies. Maybe we didn't live that life, but we could certainly aspire to it.

Many of us did lead that life and never learned the difference between good debt and bad debt. We worked hard to live the good life, but heaven help us if by some chance we lost our jobs.

We read in the newspapers about kids dropping out of school, school violence, drugs, "bad company," shootings, under-achievers, low scholastic scores and the general lack of discipline.

Why? Why are these kids in such a mess? Why aren't they behaving the way they're supposed to behave? They should be polite, good students, shouldn't they? They should be seen and not heard. Right?

You remember being a teenager, don't you? I'll bet you had your own rebellious streak. I know I did, and we all expressed that streak in different ways.

I'm sure you remember and participated in your own fashion in the disruptive 60s. Remember—

- The movie *Rebel without a Cause* with James Dean?

- Beat Generation poet Allen Ginsburg railing against the forces of materialism and conformity.

- Counterculture icon Tim Leary, who coined the phrase

"Turn on, Tune in, Drop out." He was an advocate of LSD and psychedelic drug use.

- The Watts Riots in Los Angeles, which lasted six days in 1965? There were a dozen riots in ten cities across the United States between 1964 and 1968.

- The assassinations of John and Robert Kennedy and Martin Luther King, Jr.

- The New Age?

One big difference between the rebellious state when we were youths and today is that the rebellious actions of the past where instigated and carried out by adults. They were trying, in their own fashion, to make sense of the world they lived in. They were coping with the events of that time, in that social fabric.

Today, the rebellious state is that of our youths, teenagers, and even "tweens". These kids are trying to cope in a different world and different circumstances. They're trying to find their way through a maze constructed by adults, with little, if any, positive guidance and direction. They are seeking recognition and acceptance. If they don't get it at home, they'll find it elsewhere.

When I say positive guidance and direction, I mean guidance other than the guidance of the past—be seen and not heard. Behave yourself. Basically it's a "Do as I say, not as I do" message from adults. It always has been.

Kids emulate adults. They observe how their parents act, what TV shows they watch, their habits, how they spend their money, how they act, how they relate to others, how they keep their word, how consistent they may or may not be with their choices.

Besides the overworked and overwhelmed adults at home, there are there are the adults seen on TV. The celebrities and sport stars who seem to get away with murder and with commercials that entice youngsters with unrealistic expectations and promises.

This of course leads to peer pressure because there's always some parent who will buy that "I have to have it" item which creates a pressure situation in school for the rest of the kids.

How many times have you said aloud that there are 250 channels on TV, but nothing worth watching? Yet we and our grandkids spend hours every day in front of that vast wasteland. The term was coined over 50 years ago in 1961 by Chairman of the FCC (Federal Communications Commission) Newton Minow. He said that when TV was good, it was very good, but when it was bad, it was a vast wasteland, and he felt that the industry was heading in that direction. He was right.

These kids are responding to what they observe and are taught. If they receive little or no opposition or supervision from the adults in their lives, they see their actions as acceptable and the norm.

Learning to Be Poor

The grandkids can also learn to be poor. If they pick up bad financial habits, if they see others living beyond their means and emulate these poor habits, they will have learned to live poor. It's their perception, from their observations, that what they've seen is the norm. They haven't learned because no one has taught them to stay away from bad debt and the doodads.

They have to learn the difference between a want and a need, and how they'll pay for either. Unless they're properly guided, our grandkids will take many of these false premises into adulthood and continue to perpetuate their poor financial decision making habits.

On the other hand, when taught good skills and an understanding of what it takes to become financially savvy, they'll take these concepts into adulthood and become financially independent adults.

As we look around, we find all sorts of gurus and advisors telling us what we need to do to become financially secure. We're told to "balance our portfolio and diversify", and if you don't know what or how, we'll show you how. "Give us you money and we'll make sure you're in good shape at the other end." There are newsletters, TV infomercial programs, financial channels and gurus all devoted to making you rich. Today, the Internet has more information than you need to make financial decisions.

The sponsors of this information have one primary goal and that's to make a living. They do it by dispensing financial advice and services. Very few of these individuals actually perform their own due diligence or gather their own information. Information

Teach your grandkids to avoid the following pitfalls:

- Not paying yourself first—i.e., put some money away every pay period then pay your bills.

- If you can't pay your bills after putting money aside in your savings account, you're spending too much.

- Pay off your ENTIRE credit card bill—and NEVER be late.

- Don't be suckered by fancy ads.

- Know the difference between a real need and a want.

- Ads that promise no money down and 5 years to pay with no interest are sucker bait.

- You can't get rich overnight unless you inherit the money.

- Stay away from promises of quick wealth.

and analysis is provided to them to sell to you. They're employees selling what they're told to sell. The advice is self-serving and in the interest of the seller.

These are experts we entrust with our decision making; experts, who are always quoted in the newspapers and on TV, offering their advice and wisdom. Sometimes they're right and sometimes they're wrong. Since they're the experts, they're supposed to know but many fall into the consensus department. If everyone agrees on something, it must be so. We learned about some of these experts in school. They said it was a known fact that the world was flat and the sun revolved around the earth. Everyone said so.

Today, dogmas of the past are falling by the wayside. Theories that were undisputed and were a proven fact, and therefore true, are being discredited on almost a daily basis. From medicine to science to health and technology, truths that were once held as infallible are being toppled:

- The atom was once considered the smallest particle of matter. We know that is no longer fact.

- It was a fact that after major surgery or a delivery, you'd be bed ridden for at least five to seven days. Today, the woman who delivers a child is sent home the next day, and patients are walking around within four hours after knee replacement.

- There was a time when women weren't diagnosed with heart failure, because it was a man's disease.

- The universe is no longer just stars, suns and planets. We know about black holes and that all space is filled with matter.

- Diversification is the only safe and sane way to invest in the market. Risk is bad. You'd better use due diligence on that theory.

So people find themselves giving up their decision making powers to someone else with their own agenda to keep you as a client, to make money off you. Nothing wrong with making money. But you should be the one making the decisions, and the money should be made is yours to keep.

It's okay to listen to these gurus and experts and accept the then prevalent thinking, but you have to do your own critical and analytical thinking. Be aware as changes surface in your life and with your money. Yes, you'll spend money for advice and learning, but these expenditures are your decisions.

But if no one taught you how, what do you do? How do you help your kids and grandkids become financially savvy?

> ## It takes a lot of money to buy the things you don't need!

LUANN

LUANN © GEC Inc/Distributed by United Features Syndicate, Inc.

Teach your grandkids to be VERY wary of infomercials or seminars promising huge riches with little effort.

CHAPTER EIGHT

Teach Your Grandkids to Be Financially Savvy

I t's not as difficult as it may appear at first glance.

The key is motivation. You can motivate your kids, grandkids and even yourself to become financially savvy and therefore financially secure.

Let me share a story to you.

When our eldest grandchild, Jenna, graduated from high school, my wife and I wondered what would be an appropriate graduation gift. There wasn't anything she really needed. Her parents work hard to provide the things that she and her siblings need and, on occasion, want.

On the other hand, money—cash—solves all problems. We decided that we'd give her money. She would be attending college in the fall and there are always extra expenses. We decided to give Jenna a $1,000 as a high school graduation present. That would go a long way toward giving her a jump-start. So it was settled.

But as I thought about it, I came up with another idea. We would give her a choice. She could have $1,000 cash, or she could have $25 a week for an entire year. That choice would give her

$1,300 for the year. Would she choose instant gratification or a steady cash flow? The choice would be completely hers. My wife and I had fun debating which option she would choose.

Her future decision was on my mind when I was suddenly struck with the realization that giving her money, in whatever fashion, was a continuation of the same old thing. She would receive money, only this time the occasion was graduation. The money would be spent and that would be the end of it.

An idea occurred that my wife and I could teach her to become financially savvy for life, while letting her experience and gain self-confidence and self-esteem. She'd also know that we were placing our trust in her. What greater gift could there be than that?

What we decided to do was give our granddaughter $5,000, but with strings attached. She would have to earn it by learning on her own, but with guidance, some basic economics, and financial information. She would have to acquire a different mind-set; that is, instead of being an employee and working for a paycheck her entire life, she'd have to learn to think as an investor.

We wanted her to think about working for the first 15 years of her adult life, while investing funds from this $5,000 pot so that she could become financially secure; financial security would allow her freedom to do what she was really passionate about and the security of a financially stressless life.

When she fulfilled these requirements, she would be given $5,000, but only when she could tell us how she would invest it.

The places she could NOT invest were a CD or long-term money market fund. She couldn't give it to a broker unless she told him where she wanted the money invested. She'd have to make the decision where the money was to be placed predicated on her gathering the necessary information. In other words, she'd have to learn the basics of the stock market, with direction and guidance from my wife and me, as well as her parents.

Oh, one other condition. The offer was null and void if she didn't get her check by the time she was 21! That would give her incentive, especially since she was going to be preoccupied with college life.

As an afterthought, we offered the same deal to our other six grandchildren, ranging from sixth grade to a junior in high school. Same deal, but they don't have to wait until they graduate from high school to get the money. When they fulfill the requirements, they'll get their high school graduation gift in advance. And, by the way, there was one more stipulation. They couldn't spend any of the money, any of their gains, for any other reason than to make more money.

When the grandkids graduate from college, they can't buy a car, pay for their education, put a down payment on a home (unless it's an income investment), go on vacation, pay for a honeymoon or anything else. The only thing they can do with the money, which by now should have grown substantially, is to make more money. They can't touch it for personal reasons until they turn 35. At that point, all they can spend is the money they've earned from their investments in that particular year. If they spend less than they make, then the rest returns to the pot.

That of course was our offer. You can structure yours any way you wish. The point remains that you mentor them to learn how to invest.

Don't give the hungry a fish,
teach them HOW to fish

Motivation is very strong incentive and $5,000 is a lot of cash to kids. To our surprise, our fourth grandchild, Alex, 14 years old, was the first to receive his $5,000 less than 6 months after the offer was made to him. His goal is to have $25,000 by the time he graduates from high school. Not an impossible goal by any stretch.

There are now games, programs and books available to help you teach your kids how to save money, how to make them realize the value of money and how to stop fighting over money. There's a list of these resources at the end of the book.

Realizing the value of money and learning to save money are important, but the underlying thought is still that you have to go out and work for your money. Many of these programs approach the topic from a negative (in my opinion) viewpoint that there is a lack of money, so we need to be frugal, rather than from the positive viewpoint that there is plenty of money, but you have to learn how to get it.

True, early in life your grandkids will have to work and to save, but they should also be putting money aside to add to their nest egg that they use for investments, so that they can have the satisfaction and peace of mind knowing that won't be dependent on anyone or anything for financial well-being.

Also, I'm not implying that they not work later in life because, as we all know, work can be very fulfilling. But they'll now have the luxury of making choices about what to do and when to do it. The financial needs and pressures will be greatly reduced if not completely gone.

So how do you guide a grandchild to become financially self-sufficient?

> ***Motivation and inspiration are the best teachers.***

CHAPTER NINE

Not All Kids Are Created Equal

Unless they are in someway handicapped at birth, all kids have the potential to be whatever they wish to be. That ability, however, is often quashed by our antiquated school system, which is still quagmired in the Industrial Age, and by well-meaning parents and grandparents.

Enough has been written about the need to transform our education system on how to teach our kids about coping with the dramatic changes they will face, but entrenched systems are difficult to challenge and change, and that's not the purpose of this book.

Everyone learns and absorbs information differently. Some are best at developing their skills and interests by doing, and others understand and learn best by reading.

I'm sure you've noticed that kids have their own set of priorities, and financial independence is not one of them. They are, of course, interested in money and realize they need it, but other than that they're dependent on parents, family, friends and, later on, odd jobs to get it.

The idea of learning about an obscure topic such as investing can be daunting for some kids, and younger grandchildren will need a different approach than older siblings.

Grade school kids need some basics on handling money and their allowance. They have to pay for little things they want. Yes, they'll make mistakes, but that's part of the learning process. It's also a good time to talk about wants and needs.

Teens need guidance and encouragement on a higher level, maybe a checking account and encouragement to start saving on a larger scale. In any case, watch the plastic. Is it really needed? Yes, if it's used as a teaching tool.

So not only are kids different in age, but in interests as well. Just as some are late bloomers, some will be only interested in an expanded financial education at a later age.

No matter their age, don't sell them short. Don't make the decision for them that they're too young, or aren't interested enough. Believe me, they are. It's how the lesson is presented that produces satisfactory results. It takes gentle persistence and determination. It might take a year for some youngsters to finally get on board, but they will.

Remember also that kids learn in different ways. Some want and need hands-on participation, while others prefer to read and study. Depending on their interest in money, some will grasp what you're trying to impart to them sooner than others.

The more fun the lesson, the quicker the result and the deeper the impression it has on your grandchild. That impression stays with them.

I live in Arizona. Two years ago, my two grandchildren from Flagstaff, Alex and Maisie, were visiting along with their parents. I also have two grandchildren, James and Justin, living not far from me here in the Phoenix area. Somehow, one afternoon I ended up with the four kids, ages 8, 10, 11 and 12. At one point, it was evident they were bored, nothing to do. I, just like many other grandparents started out by saying, "when I was your age......" well, you know the rest of that story.

The result of that remark was our building and painting of four scooters made out of fruit boxes (boy, were they tough to find) and skates (they're impossible to find, so we used cheap skateboards). The kids and I had a lot of fun searching for the needed supplies, building and painting the scooters, and riding them up and down the street for the next 2 days.

The scooters were taken home and never used them again. But my point is, kids can get enthused about anything, regardless of their age.

But this isn't the end of the story. Last summer, while visiting with James and Justin and their parents here in Phoenix, and just as my wife and I were leaving, the topic of the scooters came up. James and Justin wanted to know what else we could build. I was momentarily stumped, but quickly replied that we would make some gizmos.

"What are gizmos"? One of them asked.

"I don't know," I answered, "but we'll figure it out".

I've always told my grandkids that everything that happens happens because someone thought of it and made it happen. Whether it was flight, the automobile, skyscrapers, submarines, lemonade stands, someone made it happen. Everything starts with an idea, even simple things such as whether to go a movie, or watch one on TV, make a sandwich or go out to eat. Everything involves a decision. You act on every thought either by pursuing it or ignoring it. Putting off a decision is procrastination, but more on that later.

The next time I saw these two grandchildren, ages eight and ten, we started to brainstorm about what a gizmo might be. I made them understand that it could be anything they wanted it to be.

It was early summer. I'm retired, so we had several brainstorming sessions. Within two weeks my grandchildren developed a new business at which in just four days they made more money than some kids make cutting lawns all summer long.

We developed Gizmo Juice!

Gizmo Juice was nothing more than a smoothie, and the target groups were the kids and families who attended outdoor swim lessons that these two kids were part of. Simple as that.

In a nutshell, here's what they accomplished with a little guidance.

- Developed a product

- Determined their target group

- Found a source for plastic bottles in Phoenix

- Found a source for caps that would seal the bottle with a sanitary lid

- Made labels

- Made the product, sold it and took orders for next weeks swim lessons.

I, of course, had to drive them to get the eight ounce bottles. The boys were given the bottles free of charge because the company was so impressed with these two young entrepreneurs. In fact, that supplier called one of their customers in Phoenix, asking them to sell us the self-sealing bottle caps. When we went there to buy them, they were also freely given.

We then gathered up all the fresh, and some frozen, fruit from their grandmother's kitchen, took out the blender and made 12 bottles of Gizmo Juice. It took three batches of mixing various fruits, with never the same results.

I happened to have some blank labels and printed up two labels for each bottle. I took a digital photo of the two kids and put it on the front label with the words "James & Justin's Gizmo Juice". The back label had the following disclaimer—

"This special juice has been made from fresh and frozen fruit from our grandmother's kitchen. You will notice that it never tastes the same because she doesn't always have the right ingredients, and we are forced to use whatever we find. Sometimes the fruit is VERY ripe."

"If you have any complaints, see our grandmother"

The following day, the kids sold the juice for $3 a bottle. People drank it then and there, because it gets hot in Phoenix. The kids got orders for more for the following week.

They paid for all future purchases of ingredients and bottles. I asked the supplier that the kids not get the bottles free, so they paid for them.

At four separate swim practice outings, they made, clear profit, $102 each, and they enjoyed the experience tremendously. They learned a lot while having fun and even planned building a bottling plant in the desert.

My point is that kids are never too young to learn if you get them involved in the learning. Make it fun.

You'll have to find your own comfort level as well when approaching youngsters. The younger they are, the more hands on guidance will be needed. Older kids will just need guidance in the form of encouragement and overseeing. They'll also need constant reminders, prodding and support. Don't get discouraged. I learned early that their enthusiasm wasn't always in tune with my strong enthusiasm.

As I've mentioned before, I have seven grandkids and even though they've all expressed interest, not all were really ready to take me up on my offer. The attention span of the nine year old is much shorter than the high school graduate who, in reality has little time at the present to pursue her graduation gift because she's busy getting acclimated to her new surroundings in college. Being away from home, in a new environment, with new friends and in a new location, can be daunting.

I struggled with how to keep my grandchildren on course. I finally found what works for me and, perhaps, will help you in your quest to make your grandchildren financially independent.

Once I thought it through, it was simple—have the kids make financial goals for themselves. The older the kids, the grander the goals, but that's okay—nothing is out of bounds when you're day-dreaming and planning.

Goals should be beyond the immediate wants that every child has. Electronic games, iPhones, the latest gadgets and fads don't count, nor does a fancy car. The kids will have to think out of the box. Since they don't have the exposure to possibilities that you have, here are some tips to guide them –

- What would you do if you had more money than you needed? That's a thought provoking question and some answers might surprise you.

- What types of vacations would you take? All kids can relate to vacations and therefore to the larger concept of travel. There's adventure travel, cruises, visiting exotic places or just soaking up the sun on some remote beach. Travel can include such far-out places as outer space or the depths of the ocean.

- What kind of things would you like to own? All kids can relate to things such as cars and homes.

- How would you share if you had all the money in world that you needed? That's a question that will bring some surprising answers.

Their answers can become goals.

Subconsciously, they have very likely presumed that these things will be part of their adult life, they've never given them much thought. Once they start thinking about these things, they begin to set goals.

You can get kids thinking about goals by asking what they'd like to do with their lives. Here are more helpful suggestions because the kids don't have the scope of experience that you do.

- Would they like to own a business and if so, what type?

- Maybe they would like to be a scientist,

- a dancer,

- an athlete or

- an astronaut.

It makes no difference what their answers are. What matters is that they stretch their imaginations and begin think outside their experiences.

Have you noticed that kids like to do what they're good at doing, and they are good at doing what they like? When they like what they're doing, it becomes fun, whether it's ballet, baseball, math, baby-sitting, playing the viola, soccer, reading, the list goes on and on.

They may find joy and success in school and studying, or they might find joy and success in sports, music and other extracurricular activities. They might be good students, or they might learn by doing. Whatever it is, they enjoy it and are therefore good at it.

With adult support and encouragement, these kids can achieve anything.

This entire lesson on financial education can be made fun, and when it's fun, you'll succeed in teaching them to be financially savvy.

To make it fun for them, you have to make it fun for yourself as well. You have to stop being the adult and be a kid with them, share their enthusiasm, their sense of awe, their excitement at success.

You become a mutual support system for each other; the project becomes fun and successful.

As you can probably realize, this will be an ongoing exercise, as you need to talk about these things on a regular basis, otherwise interest can wane. If you keep the seriousness of the subject matter out of the conversations when you discuss various investment options, you'll succeed.

As goals are explored, achieving them becomes the normal topic of conversation.

Kids like to daydream. Why not daydream about riding camels with the Bedouin across the Sahara, taking part in a major league baseball camp, hiking the ancient Inca Trail to Machu Picchu in

Find a Way

And

Explore the Possibilities!

Peru, exploring the Lewis and Clark Trail or biking across the United States? How about being a Nobel laureate, a ground breaking scientist or even the president of your own company? There is no end to day dreams and they are all possible.

This type of brainstorming opens up their minds to all kinds of possibilities. Don't contribute to the lessening of these possibilities by creating limitations—the can't do mentality. "Everything costs money, so how are you going to pay for these dreams?" That's a limiting thought.

Here's where the concept of saving and investing comes into play. It might take weeks and even months before you get to the point of presenting your offer, especially if the kids are young. Older kids might jump on the idea quickly especially if the family is already doing some investing, i.e., stocks, rentals, etc. and the concept isn't totally foreign.

Conversations around the dinner table about finances are a wonderful way to keep the kids involved. Remind them that they can't fulfill their daydreams working paycheck to paycheck.

CHAPTER TEN

Not All Grandparents Are Created Equal

Just like grandkids, not all grandparents are created equal. No one taught us how to be grandparents, and all we have are the stereotypes from TV or from our recollections of our childhoods.

In the days of old, many grandparents were aloof, distant, overbearing, condescending and not approachable.

To get your grandkids to adopt your desire for them to become financially savvy, this approach or attitude will not work.

You have to be a kid along with your grandchildren to succeed. You need to relate to them on their terms. You can't be distant, pat them on the head and let if go at that. You can't just go to the ball game, the piano recital or the play, tell them they did a nice job and let it go at that.

Grandparents today have a difficult time relating to our grandchildren's needs and wants because we can't always identify with the new age of information and innovation. Many of us are computer literate, use e-mail and have a cell phone, but how many of us text message, download music, watch movies on handheld electronic devices, blog, use iPhones and have a MySpace or Facebook site? These things are foreign to us. We don't play electronic video games, have game cubes or listen to our music on iPods.

We were raised when a black-and-white TV was a hot-ticket item, and we were tickled pink if we were fortunate enough to get our hands on a portable radio. The generation gap between grandparents and grandchildren is huge because of technology, which is expanding exponentially.

You've heard of Moore's Law—that the number of transistors that can be inexpensively placed on an integrated circuit is increasing exponentially, doubling approximately every two years. At the same time the price is decreasing.

Heck, it was a big deal when our generation went from radio tubes to transistors!

Already, today's world is into biotechnology, biometrics, biomedicine, bioscience, photonics, genomics, nanotechnology and nanoenergy. And it's not going to slow down.

So how do we get our minds around our grandkids needs and wants when those things are so foreign to us? How do we get so involved with them that they want to participate in our dream to help them become financially savvy?

Easy—become a kid again. It means becoming openhearted and open-minded, accepting, eager and innocent. *That* they can relate to. Since grandparents too often have nothing in common with their grandkids, other than a blood relationship, the relationship at times can be perfunctory, rigid and stale.

Become an enthusiastic kid again and deal with your grandchildren as if you were their peer. Ask questions, be eager, ask for their opinion, join them in activities, go for a walk, and watch TV together. Ask them to teach you to play a video game or to text message. They'll be delighted!

When I was 62, I had the great opportunity to bicycle across the United States with my daughter, Diane. In Minneapolis, where we took a five day break while visiting with my son Bob and his family, we were interviewed on the local TV station. In response to a question posed by the reporter, my daughter said that I was nothing but a big kid. That made me feel good!

Today, my grandkids often relate to me as a kid, and as a result we all have a great rapport. We do things together. They share ideas with me, ask me questions and even offer advice. I take it as a compliment that they know they can do that and not be criticized, reprimanded or chastised.

I guess what I'm saying is that grandparents need to stop being adults for a while and should revert to being kids and enjoy the spontaneity, the wonder and excitement of experiencing and learning things in a new light.

Remember, however, that you are the adult and you can't be their best friend. But you are their mentor, a role model, something all kids need in today's world.

A change of attitude is needed. It will make it easier to interact with your grandkids on their level and become more successful in mentoring them.

You can't be a grandparent and stay out of the fray. Don't adhere to that time-honored but inappropriate adage that kids should be seen and not heard. Listen to them, engage them and honestly and enthusiastically encourage them. They'll relate better to that attitude than one that is stifled and filled with false emotion. No need to be critical or judgmental.

Kids are smart. They can see through insincerity and a false facade. They know when the accolades are sincere and heartfelt, or if they're perfunctory and shallow.

So, to be effective, become as enthusiastic with them as you will want them to become enthusiastic about this project.

In this mentoring process, think of yourself as a financial midwife, helping bring forth a new idea and teaching them some very important life skills.

They'll learn that the things they want will become less important once they can have anything they want. Think about that.

***Trust yourself.
You know more than you
think you do.***

Dr. Benjamin Spock

CHAPTER ELEVEN

Positive Steps That I Took to Become Financially Savvy

Schools don't teach you to become financially savvy—grammar school, high school or college.

However, we're all expected to make financial choices. We're bombarded with easy credit, easy mortgages and messages on why we should spend our money on various products, whether we need them or not. It's easy to be seduced and many people are. For some, it can be a slippery slope to financial dependence and even bankruptcy. Our kids and grandkids face the same bombardment of messages hyping instant gratification, at a time when they're ill-equipped to make sound decisions surrounding finances. No one has told them about analytical thinking.

Do you believe in serendipity? Do you believe that things begin to come together once you start thinking about them? They do. You just have to be aware. It happens all the time, but we're so busy, we don't connect the dots. There are times we act on these impulses, intuitions or seemingly off-the-wall information, but mostly we don't.

You might think that I have a lot of money to be able to give away $35,000 to my grandkids. When my wife and I came up with the idea, I didn't have the money, but I knew I was on my way to getting it. Things were happening that made me sure I'd have the money to give to my grandkids when they were ready.

Yeah. What things, you might be thinking? Well, they were pieces of information and ideas that were appearing. I latched on to them because I was aware that they were coming to fulfill my needs. These ideas and solutions were always out there, but I wasn't always aware of them. I wasn't always tuned in to them.

An example. I never had a lot of money, and by many standards I still don't, however, the older I get, the easier it becomes to make money without going to work for someone else.

At the moment I am writing this, I am 71 years young, on Social Security and no pension, yet I have money to go out to dinner with my wife and friends, money to travel, and money to make more money.

Five years ago, I had a Social Security check, Medicare and a modest 401k and a part time job. I had to watch my pennies. What happened?

A casual conversation with one of my kids sent my mind on a journey. My son Bob mentioned that he was investing in some property for rental income. An opportunity had arisen in his hometown and he was looking into it.

That struck a chord with me because over the years that idea had occurred to me as well, but I never acted on it. I recalled my

Dad had a three story building where he rented out one bedroom apartments, but I had no inkling if he made money, how much work was involved, etc. However, as I got older, I realized it would be nice to have some passive income. For whatever reason, like many others, I never acted on this idea. I didn't know where to begin, and I was probably afraid to get started because I didn't know anything about rental properties.

Here's where serendipity comes in. Shortly after my discussion with my son Bob, there was a full page ad in the local newspaper touting a free seminar that would teach me how to become rich in real estate. Boy, what a coincidence. I signed up to attend.

The day of the seminar arrived and by the end of the evening I had paid a discounted fee of $2995 to attend a three day seminar. Classes would be held ten days hence. I couldn't wait! Here was a chance to learn what I needed to know from an expert!

In fact I was so impatient that the following day I decided to go to my local Barnes and Noble to see if there were any books on real estate that would give me a jump-start. Boy, were there books on real estate! There were three shelves of books. Each one would give me the secrets to becoming in real estate mogul. Every book was written by an expert.

Where to start? I checked out the table of contents in several books that I thought were right for me and would steer me in the right direction. I took half a dozen or so and headed for the cafe in the back of the store to settle down and do some reading.

Several hours later, I walked out with two books. Two days later, I cancelled my three day seminar. I had learned enough from those two books to give me the information and, more importantly, the confidence that I needed to get started.

So, I acted. Within two months I purchased my first rental; within two years I purchased three more. I still have them and they've appreciated substantially, providing me with a positive passive income.

You might be thinking, "Yeah, you had the money to make the purchases". The fact is that I didn't. I had access to a 401k which was in the hands of experts but wasn't appreciating much, though I wasn't losing any principal. I realized it wouldn't take very many years to exhaust my funds once my mandatory drawdown began at 70 ½ . I took a leap of faith and slowly liquidated my 401k to buy my four rentals with a normal 20% down payment.

My point is that I made some basic decisions and acted on them.

As you all know, the road to hell is paved with good intentions. You have to act. I did, and these acts have improved my financial situation. I acted because I became aware of opportunities that presented themselves and then I began to look for more. They are fairly easy to find. I now get a lot of satisfaction just looking for them and making some of them come to fruition. I became motivated to do more and I gained self-confidence. I didn't pay anyone to teach me.

And so it is with your kids and grandkids. You can motivate them to learn to do the same with a few simple steps.

CHAPTER TWELVE

Steps to Take to Make Your Grandchildren Financially Savvy

So what can you do to make your grandkids financially savvy, especially since you may not feel competent to share knowledge? You may have had your stockbroker suggest and then purchase your stocks, or you might own mutual funds you haven't looked at for years. Or you may not be invested in the stock market. Not everyone is.

Yearly, these advisors send you an overview of your positions. Outlined in a triangle are your areas of risk, of your diversification in growth, value, small, or large-cap stocks. They might suggest that you tweak your positions to reflect reducing your risk as you get older. If you don't do anything, don't make any changes, they don't care.

You're responsible for making the final decisions on your investments, but many of us have relied on the advice of others to make those decisions.

The financial landscape, however, is changing. Full-service brokers that charge huge fees for every transaction are slowly falling by the wayside. Flat fee Internet trading is gaining popularity and you don't have to be a day trader to use that tool.

My 14 year old grandson Alex, is being tutored by his dad, Paul, on monitoring his small portfolio on the Internet.

Have you noticed all the mail you're getting about free seminars that want to acquaint you with various financial products—annuities, reverse mortgages, self-directed IRAs, how to save taxes on your 401k withdrawals, how to leave more money for your loved ones—and the list goes on?

These seminars are marketing tools to introduce you to new concepts regarding savings concepts that you might not have been aware of. This information is priceless, though it may not be for you. I like attending these seminars because they're a source of ideas for me.

The point here is that the financial landscape is changing and how you manage your money is changing. One thing that hasn't changed is that someone is always there, willing to handle your funds for you.

So, where do you begin? How can you help and guide your grand-children, if you yourself don't feel informed or knowledge-able? You have to stay in step with them, since you'll be helping to guide them. As I mentioned earlier, motivation and involvement are key.

First some basics:

Throw out the piggy banks and get rid of allowances all together! If these concepts really worked, we would all be in a better financial place! Here are some facts:

Fact #1: The history of the piggy bank is based in poverty and supports a "save to spend" mentality with our kids and grandkids in a world where coins are not truly valued

Fact #2: Even if parents pay their kids an allowance, the allowance is inconsistent, under valued and is usually considered "pocket money" where kids only learn one thing … how to spend.

Fact #3: Kids do learn about money. They learn about money by watching their parents work with money and listening to conversations their parents have about money. Kids learn their parents' money habits—whether good or bad. And in a world of instant gratification where you can simply swipe a card and get what you want, there's no wonder kids think that money comes from the "magic wall" at the bank (also known as the ATM Machine)! Younger kids think that you simply put a card into the magic wall and money comes out. They have no concept of how the money even made it into that "magic wall" or the connection between parents working, earning money and depositing money into the bank.

For a systematic solution that teaches kids how to manage money before they start to earn it, consider purchasing the KidsWealth Money Kit at www.KidsWealth.com. The KidsWealth

Money Kit teaches kids how to manage money in the five key areas of wealth, planning, learning, having fun doing it and becoming an angel. An angel is the concept of giving money to help others in need.

Graduate to a savings account. A savings account is an abstract idea in many ways. As tweens, kids learn to handle abstract ideas and won't feel that they are giving their money away to a bank. By now, in school, they have learned multiplication and can understand how interest works.

Introduce budgeting. Kids in middle school should understand that their money is limited and should be able to differentiate between a need and a want. Funds are limited. What do you want to spend, if anything?

Open a Roth IRA. By the time kids are 15 or 16, they have part-time or summer jobs. Have them place some of those earned funds in a tax-free Roth IRA. You can match what they save. Watch those saving grow, and they can be withdrawn tax free. Check with your accountant about these benefits. You will be astounded.

Before your grandchild goes off to college, it might be a good idea to introduce them to credit cards so they understand the dangers of not paying off their balance each and every month. They, of course, are responsible for the payment of these debits out of their funds.

Here are some other basic steps to encourage kids to become financially savvy.

1. Steer them to books that will help them get an idea of the changing world, how they have to change their mind-set, how they have to learn to think for themselves and out of the box. Out of the box means beyond a job. They see their parents going to work, to their jobs. You want their imaginations to soar to what *they* could do if they didn't have a job.

A number of books available and a suggested reading list appears at the end of this book. However, for young minds I recommend Robert T. Kiyosaki's book *Rich Dad/Poor Dad for Teens*. This book is geared for teenagers, though younger kids can understand the concepts. It's perfect for the youngster who learns best by studying. *Rich Dad's Rich Kid, Smart Kid* is for the adult, to stress how important it is to invest in your kids.

The basic idea presented in these books is slanted toward income and how you earn it.

A. As an employee, where you receive a paycheck in exchange for doing your work. Here you're dependent on someone else for your income. You don't show up, you don't get paid. Lose your job, lose your paycheck. In this position, you work for your money. Believe me, your boss won't make you rich.

B. As a self-employed individual, i.e, a doctor, lawyer, real estate agent, Mary Kay sales person, etc. In this situation, you are your own boss, but you basically have bought your job. You can't be fired, but if you don't work, you don't get paid. You have more leeway, but you're still tied down to wherever you go to work, even if it's at home. In this category, you're still working for your money.

C. As a business owner. This is where you begin to take control over your income. You have others do the work and you provide vision and guidance, as well as contribute work, but you're free of the basic chores of an employee or a self-employed individual. In this scenario, you have your money working for you in the guise of employees, who are making money for you and therefore improving your financial situation. It's hard work establishing and running a business, and it isn't for everyone. The rewards, however, can be huge. As a business owner, you're building an asset that can bring a large financial gain at some future period in time.

D. As an investor. Your income is passive income. That is, you don't depend on earning it from work. You earn money from investments that produce a cash flow and appreciate. You're responsible for keeping track of your investment's performance and spend some time looking for other opportunities. With a laptop and the Internet, you can do this from your condo in Hawaii or any other place of your choosing. Your money works for you; you don't work for your money.

Believe me, your grandkids will have no difficulty in understanding these concepts and will very quickly identify with where they want to be in that quadrant.

2. To help everyone conceptualize the ideas presented in his books, Robert T. Kiosayki has developed board games called *Cashflow 101©*, and *Cashflow for Kids©*. Similar to *Monopoly®*, both are much more interactive and instructive as decision making exercises. In these games, you are given an occupation, pay rate, family and monthly expenses associated with that life. Your goal, with the aid of money making opportunities, which you decide to accept or reject, is to extract yourself from the Rat Race onto the Investment Track. The games teach critical and analytical thinking and decision making. You reap the results, which can include either bankruptcy or the quality life we all seek, through your decisions. A very powerful tool, indeed.

You can find the game on eBay or www.RichDad.com. The books can also be obtained at any book store.

This board game works especially well for kids who learn best by doing. The game forces you to plan, to think, to take risks, or avoid them, but in the end, whether you win or lose, and you have to take responsibility for your decisions.

3. Once the kids have read the book and you've played the game several times, (I play with my grandchildren. They really enjoy it when they win) their next project is to learn, in real life, about the investments that were part of the game.

When we were an agricultural society, everything we needed to know to survive was in our heads—what seeds to plant, when to plant, when to reap, how to identify good soil. We learned to

Are You Ready for...

One piece of advice you can offer your grandchildren is that there are always two opposing views to any situation, and that includes investing.

On the same day, someone will tell you the market is going up, and another advisor will tell you it's heading down.

Some authors and gurus will swear that the stock market is the only way to financial success; others will tout the virtues of real estate.

There are opposing views as to the direction of any financial trend. Is gold headed up in the long run or not, is the trend of the market up or down, is real estate finished as an investment vehicle, or is it in a temporary slump, poised to go higher?

Even the experts don't see eye to eye.

understand the weather; we knew when the crops needed to be watered. We knew what was edible, what wasn't, we understood the seasonal changes.

Today that's a lost art. Today, everything you need to know to survive is outside your head. There's just too much information to keep everything but the basics in your hard drive, the brain.

Today, you don't even have to go to the library to get information. It's on the Internet. The Internet is a very powerful instrument. You can learn anything, buy anything, and even contribute to writing of an encyclopedia. That's where your grandkids will go to seek information on the basics of financial investments. They can learn about the stock market, mutual funds, ETFs (Exchange Traded Funds), derivatives, currency trading, bonds, commodities and so much more.

Earlier in the book, when I told the story of my grandfather's venture into the stock market, I wasn't sure of the name of the oil company. I quickly did a search and found my answer. Just about any information is available on the Internet.

Money is to be made in bull and bear markets, in boom and bust real estate markets and in inflationary or deflationary times. This is where critical and analytical thinking come into play.

Not that your grandkids have to know all this stuff. For the present, they just have to be aware of what the stock market is and, when they want more information they know where to find it. You can go to Barnes and Noble or any other book store, check through their financial or investment sections, pick out some books on investing or finance, take them to the cafe in the back of the store and skim through these books. You can purchase what you want, or go to the library. I take my grandkids whenever possible, and we all enjoy our discussions and quality time, not to mention the hot chocolate.

I didn't demand that my grandkids become experts on investing, just that they understood what's out there—what's the DOW, the NASDAQ, the Wilshire 5000 etc. And that they became familiar with the basic language of finance, i.e., p.e. ratios, equity, debt, short sales, options, etc. They don't have to understand everything at once, but they have to understand what a mutual fund is and what is the function of a stockbroker, a financial advisor, and the difference between the two. They have to learn, over time, the language of investing, whether it's stocks, bonds, real estate or commodities.

In my opinion, the best print source for basic investment ideas and understanding financial investments is the *Investor's Business Daily.* The newspaper provides excellent daily information to help any individual make intelligent decisions, and provides ideas that can be examined.

Most importantly, the newspaper provides daily columns on how to invest, how to set guidelines, how to understand the symbols associated with the stock market. The paper grades each stock for quick analysis, another invaluable tool.

Investors Business Daily also teaches you how to analyze a stock and provides practical advice to keep you on track.

There's a lot of good information on the web, in books and articles, newspapers, etc, but here's where you make a difference.

Depending on the source, most financial information is biased and slanted to whatever product or service someone is selling. That's not bad thing, but critical and analytical thinking has to come into play for you to make a decision as to the validity of the product for your particular need. Read, but verify.

Let the kids do what they're good at—research on the Internet. Let them pick a few stocks to purchase. If they don't know where to start, they can begin with familiar companies—those that make the iPods, their jeans, their video games, their sporting equipment or the family car.

Let them defend their choices of stock, let them tell you how long they plan to keep them, what the parameters will be and why. Then let them decide how they'll purchase those shares—which Internet trading account or possibly your broker. They'll need your guidance, but it's their decision. Don't negate their decision. If you feel the choice is a poor one, explain why but let them stick with it if they want to.

4. Another avenue for investing for income is real estate. In many ways, it's more rewarding than the stock market, which sometimes, even with all its pundits and experts, is similar to going to a casino. You have to be on top of your stock investments. In the

medium term, these investments will not provide the passive stream of income you're seeking to make you financially independent.

You'll hear two sides to the theory that more money has been made in real estate than in any other venue. In my opinion, an accurate statement.

Our population is growing and people need to live somewhere; food has to be produced and grown somewhere. That somewhere is land. Since it is not being made any more, it keeps increasing in value as more people need it to build a house, or grow some food. The population of the United States will continue to grow.

Obviously, not all land is created equal. It might be nice to own the Grand Canyon, but who wants a fissure running through the middle of their 10 acre land investment.

There's money to be made in rentals, new properties, manufactured homes, fix-and-flips, distressed properties, apartments and condos, commercial property, malls, office buildings and parking lots. You can own paper (mortgages), have options on properties, or even be a lender. There are times and places for each of these strategies.

You have to know where to start and you usually start with a single property that can be your home for two years, at which time you can sell it and save on taxes, or you can convert it into a rental.

Real estate investing doesn't always require a lot of money to get started. You can invest in REITs (**Real Estate Investment**

Trusts), which can be purchased just like stocks. REITs can also be purchased though mutual funds.

Also, check the business section of any large city newspaper. If you live in a small town, you can check it out on the Internet. Look for those ads that will give you in 10% to 16% return on your money (in 2007, anyway). The money you invest is usually used by a real estate development company for the development of land that they own. The developer needs your money to give him leverage when he goes to the bank for more money. There are various scenarios to this, but your money is secured by the real estate. These companies offer short seminars so that you can ask questions and make intelligent decisions.

If you can't take advantage of one of these seminars because of your location, check out the websites of these companies. If you can not find such an ad or company, I suggest you check out the website of the Red Door Group (www.RedDoorGroupInc.com) and click on their Investment Opportunities section.

If you choose to follow the real estate option, and eventually you will, find a real estate broker that deals with investors. These agents understand what you're attempting to achieve and are tuned in to your needs. They know that investors, over time, end up purchasing more than one property, and meeting your demands will make you a repeat customer. They are an excellent source of information and it's all free.

How do you find a real estate broker who deals with investors? Just ask any broker. If they don't, they can usually suggest someone. A caveat here. Some brokers might be tempted to say yes, so ask them if they own any investment properties. If they do, ask them who manages the properties. Ask about the strength of the rental market for individual residences. If they're not comfortable answering these questions, move on to the next agent.

It's always good to use a qualified real estate agent because they work for free. They don't get paid until there's a sale, and then they are paid by the seller, not you.

Another interesting and very useful option is to take the kids to those free seminars that are constantly being offered. You can attend seminars on real estate, the stock market, eBay, Internet marketing and on the virtues of raising llamas. There is no obligation, and they can be very informative and full of ideas. The idea for this book came from one of those seminars.

Again, there are options. Take your grandkids and check out the Barnes and Noble or any other book store in your neighborhood. Sit down with a coffee and browse the books for ideas. The information is free and it can help start your grandchild toward making their first million.

Of course, your grandkids can't do this on their own. This is where your motivation and the carrot of money come into play. You and their parents need to be involved in nurturing this new adventure.

Have casual conversations about finances (their finances specifically), what's happening in the financial world, credit cards, financial responsibility, choices and, of course, decision making.

Encourage them, question them and support them. Believe me, they're eager students when it comes to money especially when they're part of the decision making process.

Most important is that they act on their decisions. Nothing gets done without acting. A decision without action is not a decision, it's a thought.

And this is the final part of the kid's training, acting on their decisions. I want to know where my grandkids will invest their money. Since they won't have enough to invest in a rental at this time, I'll want to know what stock, mutual fund, REIT or ETF they will invest in and why.

I will not exercise any veto power on their decision, though I'll try and help guide them, and I'll want to know what results they expect from their decision and in what time frame. Also, what is Plan B should the investment eventually not meet their criteria.

As I mentioned earlier, they won't be able to touch any of this money until they are 35. I won't put this money in any trust or controlled account. It's theirs to manage, to learn, and to earn.

One last thing. Not all kids will be on the same page at the same time. They have their own agendas. Making money is intriguing, but sometimes the idea of learning sits on the back burner.

This is where the mentoring, the prodding, the example setting come in. They need you to get started, but once they have, get out of their way.

Motivation

If you have several grandchildren living miles apart and you don't see them very often, how do you keep them motivated? They bought into *your* idea, now how to you help them adopt it as *their* goal?

Recently, my wife Lorraine, and I were going to see Maisie, our granddaughter in Flagstaff, dance in a ballet recital. It was one of these events that only attract parents and occasionally, grandparents.

Approaching an intersection, I noticed a couple of youngsters holding a sign and jumping up and down, waving to the passing cars. No doubt about it, they were excited and enthused.

"CAR WASH", the sign read in large letters.

Fifty feet farther down the road were two more youngsters, shouting and waving. Their sign said that they were eighth graders from the local elementary school.

The third and final sign read "FREE CAR WASH— Donations Accepted and Appreciated."

Around the corner was a line of cars. There were four stations and they were all busy with youngsters scrambling to wet the cars with a hose, soap them, rinse them and dry them. All of the kids in this project were motivated, and they were having fun.

Have you ever noticed kids selling lemonade at their lemonade stand? There are always several kids, some waving you down, others pouring your lemonade and someone taking your money. These kids are excited to sell you their product. They're motivated and they're having fun.

I'm sure you've seen adults standing on a corner with a "SALE" or a "GOING OUT OF BUSINESS" sign, directing you to a furniture sale, to an automobile dealership, to a model home opening. Did those people look excited? Heck no! They were bored out of their minds. They were there for a paycheck and couldn't wait for the time to pass. They weren't enthused and their motivation was an immediate need. They had a pressing bill to pay. There was no fun in what they were doing. The job was done out of necessity.

Have you on some occasion observed your grandchild coming home from a baby-sitting job, or from some other odd job and counting their money? They did whatever it was that earned them the money because they were motivated. Their motivation was something they wanted to purchase, some want or need they had and wanted to fulfill. They are motivated.

Ask your grandkids what motivates them, what excites them, what turns them on. The answer will always be the same—**FUN**.

They like to do things that are **fun**. Dig a little deeper.

They like to play video games because that's where the action is and they can identify with a character. It's **fun**!

They like to read for **fun** because they can mentally place themselves into the adventure and identify with a character.

They like to play sports, to be in the band, to participate in extra-circular activities because these things are **fun**. You've seen kids get very excited at school sporting events. They're excited because they identify with **their** team.

Kids do well in school because the subject matter is **fun**. The teacher has found a way to make it **fun**.

Through all these activities, kids identify with success, self-esteem, recognition, achievement, and self-satisfaction. And that motivates them because it is **fun** and they like the way it makes them feel.

Come to think of it, don't we all do best at things that are **fun** for us? Things that we like to do?

Therefore, the motivation to encourage your grandchildren is to make the project **FUN**!

I checked with my grandkids about this. Something is **fun** because it's **interesting,** and it's **interesting** because it's **challenging**.

It doesn't necessarily follow that all **challenging** things are **fun**. Learning math or science, playing a musical instrument, sports, and many other things are **challenging** but are not always **fun** to many kids.

They're not **fun** for many reasons, but primarily it's because, for whatever reason, there's no **interest** in that particular study or sport.

So how do you make investing **fun**? Basic economics can be pretty dull. Studying market trends and company performance, or searching for investments can be as much **fun** as watching grass grow.

Well, as I mentioned earlier, kids aren't created equal and what motivates one will not necessarily work on another. It's a difficult hurdle to overcome, especially if you're not living close to your grandchildren where you can have a more direct personal impact. So what do you do?

Let me share with you three possible scenarios. All of them are one-size-fits all suggestions. And best of all, kids eight or nine can participate and learn with the older grandchildren.

Scenario #1—E-mail

Just about everyone uses e-mail. Tell the grandkids, those that live close by and those that live further away, that as far as this investment project is concerned, you'll all communicate by e-mail, or instant messaging or blogging. You can interface with them on MySpace or Facebook

Did I loose you there? Let me quickly explain.

Instant messaging is real-time Internet communication. It allows instantaneous communication between a number of parties simultaneously, by transmitting information quickly and efficiently, featuring immediate receipt of acknowledgment or reply. In certain cases, instant messaging involves additional features which make it even more popular, i.e., to see the other party. by using webcams, or to talk directly for free over the Internet.

A **blog** (combination of we**b** and **log**) is a web site where entries are written in chronological order and commonly displayed in reverse chronological order. Blog can also be used as a verb, meaning to maintain or add content to a blog.

MySpace and Facebook are just two of the many social network sites on the web. Kids use them to communicate, share ideas, and stories and much more with their friends. Ask them and they'll share with you how it works.

Believe it or not, your grandkids are aware of these possibilities and might already be involved in them. Involve them in creating a communication system that fits their skills. They'll teach you along the way, and because it will be **fun** for them, they will do a good job at it.

This form of communication will serve two functions. One, it will give you the ability to offer advice and counseling in an abstract yet concrete way to ALL the kids at the same time. Some seeds of wisdom will fall by the wayside, but some will germinate and ideas will begin to form.

All the grandkids concerned with this investment project will be in the loop. Everyone will get the same message, the same information. Whenever there are responses, everyone is copied.

Ideas can be exchanged, strategy discussed and investment opportunities explored. Some of the grandkids will be more involved than others, but that's where you come in, to support, ask questions of, and make suggestions to those who are less participatory.

Many kids need constant encouragement as they find their voices to express their ideas. Recognize this, and let them know they shouldn't fear participating or voicing opinions because of a lack of knowledge. They're there to learn. And so the **fun** begins. Get their parents involved as well.

A very important aspect of this is updating everyone on individual progress. When one of the kids finishes a portion of their assignment, i.e, reading the book, playing the game or visiting the web sites, they announce it to all via e-mail. When one of the kids gets his or her check, they outline, for everyone, how they plan to invest it. With proper guidance, this success will motivate the others.

The grandchild who's first to receive his investment pot will now become a key figure in the interplay via e-mail. They will become, in a surrogate way, mentor, as they discuss their strategies and share their successes and failures.

You, as mentor, will use that success to encourage the others. The kids will rise to the challenge.

Scenario #2—An Investment Club

An idea that I used successfully was the formation of an investment club comprised of only the grandchildren.

In this scenario, all the grandkids contribute a fixed amount and collectively get involved in the investment of those funds.

Let me explain how this worked for me.

To keep the kids involved, especially those living a great distance from me, I had the grandkids pool $500 each. This resulted in a pot of $3,500. The idea was to take that money and invest it in the stock market.

The SECONDARY goal was to make money. The FIRST goal was to get the kids excited about their ability to make decisions that would influence the outcome of their investment, and to monitor the results.

What I did, and you can do whatever suits your needs and the abilities and ages of your grandkids is this—

1. I opened up an Internet trust account, in the name of the kids, with an online trading company. I was the trustee and the one who would be making the trades.

2. I divided the stock market into 4 investment segments

   • **Retail**—because the kids can associate with favorite products, such as clothing, electronics, etc.

- **Energy**—because I've found that my grand-children can associate with alternative energy.

- **Technology**—because nanotech, biotech, neurotechnology and information technologies are all driving components of our future

- **Health**—The aging of the boomer generation and the chances coming in this sector demand that it be investigated.

3. Within each segment, I identified 3 promising stocks.

4. With guidance from their parents and me, each child picked any three stocks that they wished. They then had to research those stocks and tell the rest of us why they though that their choices should be purchased by the group.

The group would then vote on which stocks to purchase. Our goal was to purchase 25 to 50 shares of three or four companies.

5. Each grandchild was responsible for checking on the stocks on a regular basis, if not every day. We would be in contact on a weekly basis (via e-mail) unless there was an important development. We had previously set up sell instructions with the broker to protect ourselves from unacceptable losses.

Not many kids have $500 lying around to set up such an investment club, but having them get the money was much easier than I first imagined.

I put in the first $100 and they were responsible for the other

> ## *A decision without action is just a thought.*

$400.00. I gave them some suggestions on getting the money, and they all had it within several of weeks!

They got their parents to contribute; they did a sales job on aunts and uncles and on their other grandparents. Some even covered any shortfall with their own savings. They were excited! This was going to be fun!

The one thing we did not do was set an expiration date for this investment club. If anyone wanted to leave, they would get their share of any funds—one-seventh of the pot. No one has yet left, though any money they earn from their decisions is theirs to do as they wished.

A different variation on this idea is a family investment club.

Just as the name suggests, the entire family is involved in financial discussions. The grandparents, as well as Mom and Dad sit down on a regular basis and discuss their investments and ideas for other moneymaking ventures. The kids are included, and encouraged to participate and share their strategies and research. They can even do some research for the elders as part of their education.

Scenario #3—Individual Investment Accounts

An alternative to the above option is to allow the grandkids to establish and control their own accounts.

Get Involved and the Kids Will Respond.

©Bill Keane, Inc King Features Syndicate

With the $500, they have to pick a company, investigate the stock, evaluate the risks and rewards, and make their choices.

You'll still mentor them with suggestions and direction, but this option puts more responsibility on them. It will more quickly expose them to the language of the stock market, to new and emerging possibilities in new technology, new ideas, innovations and even career interests. Over time, they'll learn to think for themselves, seek their own answers, become creative and fully engaged.

The grandkids might even seek suggestions from older cousins or siblings via e-mail, and I would suggest that you encourage such an exchange.

You, as the grandparent, the mentor, will help them whenever and wherever they need guidance and motivation. Literally, you will be by their side, asking about their investments and letting them know that you're VERY interested in their success.

You may not think you know enough to help them but you know more than they do, and when you get immersed in the process, they'll help you as much as you help them.

Steps to Take

- Teach them to understand the difference between working for their money as opposed to having their money work for them.

- You know your grandkids best. Help them discover their talents and skills by becoming involved with them.

- With the input of your grandchildren, decide which of the described scenarios will work best for your family.

- If you're not personally involved in the stock market, or feel overwhelmed, take the time to open a small account with an on-line trading company and learn how easy it can be.

CHAPTER THIRTEEN

Ideas for Working With Limited Funds

Not everyone has $5,000 to invest in this project, but that doesn't mean that you can't get started.

Kids get a lot of money over the course of a year, but very little, if any, is long-term goal orientated. Some kids may know that money is being put away for college, but that's fairly ambiguous to them. They don't see it, they don't realize how much college costs, so it's something they may be aware of, but have no control over.

Some kids have a savings account they use to purchase the more expensive items they may want, i.e., electronic games, iPods, iPhones and who knows what else. With one purchase, most, if not all, of their savings evaporate and they start saving again. It's like chasing yourself around a tree.

This project is about having your grandkids be aware of money, of earning it through proper and well thought out investments.

However, aside from investing, they also need to learn the basics:

- Savings accounts,

- Checking accounts,

- Balance their checkbook,

- Manage debt,

- Pros and cons of credit cards,

- Differentiating between want and need,

- Creating a financial plan.

- They need to learn how to open, navigate and use an Internet trading account.

The more they learn to manage their funds and make decisions and allocations of funds, the better able they will be to make sound financial decisions. The sooner they learn to make these decisions, the sooner they can learn to be investors.

Not to be redundant, but proper and well thought out investments will provide the grandkids with the ability to make choices free of financial stress and help provide them with a life they choose to lead.

Today's kids might live to see the next century. We should help them plan so that they can afford to live that long.

Sources of Funds

As I've mentioned earlier, this should be a family project, with parents helping guide the kids along the way. After all, they see

their kids every day and can answer their questions and help prod them along.

Parents

Parents can also be a source of seed money. They can add to the pot rather than spending all the money on gifts during holidays and other occasions. Tell the kids that a portion of any monies they receive as gifts has to be put into the investment piggy bank and eventually into a savings account.

Other Grandparents

The other grandparents can also be invited to make a contribution to the pot. They're just as interested as you in the welfare and well-being of their grandkids.

Inheritance

One way or another, the upcoming generation will reap a huge financial windfall through inheritance. A portion of those funds could be used to start your grandchildren's financial education. Consider giving them a part of their potential inheritance in advance, the way I gave my grandkids their graduation gift in advance. They, of course, have to earn it as determined by you and with your help. Wouldn't you rather know they're capable of managing those funds by getting them started now?

Some inheritances are in a trust, so that a minor doesn't have access to those funds until they reach a certain age, as determined by the deceased. They might receive these funds when they're 21 or 35, and then spend most of the money on "stuff", leaving little if any funds for savings or investments.

Wouldn't it serve a better purpose if they received a small portion of that inheritance when they're still minors so they could learn to invest? When they get the jackpot, they're already attuned to investing.

Kids Contributions

The kids can take a portion of the money they receive from family and friends as gifts and add it to the pot. Also, they can contribute on a regular basis from allowances and money earned doing various jobs.

Matching Funds

As an incentive to your grandchildren, offer to match any monies of their own that they put into the pot. You can match them dollar for dollar or some percentage of what they put away.

Yearly Contributions

Another source of potential funds is for you and your spouse to add incremental yearly amounts to your grandchild's pot. You set any guidelines you wish on this. It can be a surprise, possibly based on last year's performance of their investment portfolio, a percentage of what they have saved, or a fixed amount.

Tax Law

Remember that you, as an individual, can give away tax free up to $12,000 to each grandchild you have each and every year if you wish. Your spouse can also match tax free any amount up to $12,000.

Stock

You can give the kids shares of stock. We'll talk about that in the next section.

However, remember—the money in the pot can't be used for anything other than investing. No toys, gifts, iPods, computer games, electronic gizmos or as a down payment on a car.

They can't pay for their college education, spend it on a trip or vacation, pay for their wedding, honeymoon or even for a deposit on a home, unless it is a PLANNED investment property.

Investment Ideas for Small Amounts of Money

Where can you invest if you only have several thousands dollars or less to start with? How do you get that nest egg to start growing?

Growth in dollars will be slow at first. It's like learning to crawl before you can join the track team. At first, depending on the amount of funds, your options will be limited; however, with patience, perseverance and study, the pot can grow quite large. In fact, once everyone is infected with the idea of saving and watching as the pot grows, they'll want to add more funds to the pot, just to get started with some serious investing.

Let the kids be as aggressive as possible at this stage, since you'll want as much growth as possible. If they remember the first rule of investing, don't lose the principal, they'll do fine.

Cash

If you plan to do as I did, provide a large lump sum of money, remember that before the kids get it, they have to become somewhat financially literate. They have to have a basic understanding of the financial markets and investment options.

Once they've satisfied you that they're truly interested in the project by taking the time to learn and fulfill your requirements to receive their funds, they now have to make a decision: What do I want to do with my money? It can be invested in the stock market, in treasury or corporate bonds.

Where stocks are concerned, a trading account can be set up with any of the Internet brokerage accounts that charge as little as $7 per trade. Have the kids check out whether they want corporate stocks or treasury bonds. Money market accounts don't pay much interest, but they're a good place to park your money for a short period of time between investments. Higher rates might be found in out of state banks. All this information is available on the Internet, the choice of research for all youngsters.

My personal choice would be to have the grandchild open an Internet online trading account and buy shares in a company or two with whatever limited funds they may have.

If you have $10,000, seriously consider responding to one of the private real estate ads that can lead to a 10% to 16% return on your money. The funds are usually tied up for a year, though sometimes longer. They're medium risk, and return twice as much as a CD. There is more information on this in the Real Estate section later in this chapter

Making a decision to purchase stock, mutual funds or place the money in a Money Market fund is a function of risk tolerance. Usually, the higher the perceived risk, the higher the return. Stocks are volatile, and therefore have a potential for a great return, or a quick loss if they aren't monitored.

Risk, by the way, is starting to invest too late and learning the lessons late in life. If you try to play catch up, you have to take greater risks because of the shortened time frame that you have to work with. It's also a time when you become risk-adverse, because you don't want to lose what you have.

The younger you are, the greater the tolerance for risk, because there's time to recover from losses. Better to learn these lessons earlier than later.

Mutual funds are less volatile, and Treasury bonds and CD's provide a predetermined and guaranteed return with usually very little risk. Usually, low risk equals low return; however, that doesn't have to be the case. Check out the information in the real estate section of this chapter.

I think you'll find that your grandkids, at first, will have a low tolerance for risk, as they will afraid of making mistakes. They'll be willing to take on more risk as they gain confidence.

This isn't a bad thing because they'll learn not to be afraid to explore new avenues. Guide them, but don't discourage them. It's better to make mistakes now, when the stakes are smaller and there's plenty of time to recover.

That's why grandkids need to learn how to monitor their investments, learn their comfort level with risk and act accordingly. The more they do this, the more comfortable they will become. As they become adults, they'll be well on their way to thinking and acting as investors, ready to try new investments as their portfolio grows.

Stocks

You might decide that your contribution, or that of some other family member, to this project, should be stock. That's a great way to get started because you can explain why you purchased the stock, and after it's transferred to their name help them set some goals as to when to sell or buy more. A stock is something the kids will enjoy tracking on the Internet every day. It's theirs—the account will have their name on it and they'll become motivated as they monitor the activities of the market, their stock or some other stock they may become interested in.

Obviously, they should have a Plan B for the stock. There has to be an exit strategy, i.e., when to sell. At some point, it will be sold and where will the money be invested? There should be a chosen stock or two waiting in the wings to be purchased. Or, perhaps, they may want to add to their position.

There are a lot of other investing alternatives in the market as well, but that's beyond the scope of this book.

You've probably noticed on financial news stations that there are usually two views represented for the same question. That should tell you that even the experts don't agree, and you have to make your own decisions to the best of your ability. I again suggest **IBD**, (*Investment Business Daily*). They also have an excellent website (www.Investors.com) which teaches you how to make valid analytical decisions. It's an excellent resource.

There are pros and cons to investing in the market just as there are pros and cons to any investment. Teach the kids the importance of due diligence and to think of every investment as a long-term project and not a get-rich-quick deal, even though you may be in a particular stock for a relatively short time.

Penny Stocks

One overlooked area is investments are "Penny Stocks". These investments are so-called because of their value, or lack of value.

In the U.S. financial markets, the term *penny stock* commonly refers to any stock trading outside one of the major exchanges (NYSE, NASDAQ, or AMEX), and is often considered unworthy. However, the official SEC definition of a penny stock is a low-priced, speculative security of a very small company, regardless of market capitalization or whether it trades on a securitized exchange (like NYSE or NASDAQ) or an "over the counter" listing service, such as the OTCBB or Pink Sheets.

Many new investors are lured to the appeal of penny stocks

due to the low price and potential for rapid growth which may be as high as several hundred percent in a few days.

However, these stocks may lack liquidity—a lack of demand, resulting in manipulation by management, market makers and third parties.

Fraud is found in these areas, especially on the internet and unwanted 3rd party e-mails touting huge gains.

I have purchased shares of a very reputable home builder who had fallen on hard times during the recent housing crash and had to declare bankruptcy. The stock fell from a high of $30 dollars to a low of .09 cents over the course of 15 months. As of this writing the stock has risen to .22 cents. A nice gain of 240%. You don't need huge amounts of money to make money, but you do have to do some due diligence.

You might want to check out www.PennyStocks.com and click on the "Free Stuff" button, which will lead you to some basic information about penny stocks. The site is operated by a reputable individual, frequently quoted in the financial press and seen of TV.

Check the Suggested Resources page for a book about penny stocks. It might be an area to investigate if you are working with a small amount of funds.

Real Estate

You may believe you need a lot of money to invest in real estate, but that's not necessarily true. Since we're speaking of limited funds, I'm not going to get into the no-money-down get rich quick gimmicks. At this point, be aware of them, but, that is not the way to go.

I had mentioned earlier companies that offer up to 10% to 16% (2007) return on your money. These companies secure your short term funds (usually up to three years) with real estate. If you look in the business section of any large newspaper, you'll see several ads offering seminars on these products. Attend one. If possible, take your older grandkids to listen and learn. They probably won't grasp everything, but they'll be exposed to new ideas.

This is a viable route to take. It will give you a good return with acceptable risk and a moderate investment.

If you can't take advantage of one of these seminars because of your location, check out the websites of these companies. If you can't find such an ad or company, I suggest that you check out the website of the Red Door Group (www.RedDoorGroupInc.com) and click on their Investment Opportunities section.

Red Door Group is the fund-raising arm and represents a group of Right Place Properties in a very worthy mission. The Right Place mission is simple—renovate existing real estate to create quality, affordable residential properties that provide mutually profitable opportunities for buyers, employees, associates, investors and owners.

At some future date, as your funds increase, you might want to consider becoming either a commercial or a residential landlord. Becoming a landlord is overwhelming to many people and they prefer to avoid those responsibilities. Be aware that there are management companies that will manage that property—find tenants, collect rents, do repairs and pay the taxes for you.

Again, this is not the scope of this book, but be aware that these options exist.

Teach your grandkids
Rule #1 of Investing:
Don't lose the principal,
your seed money.

Tax Liens

Tax liens are attempts by a county to collect delinquent real estate taxes. After a year, when a property owner fails to pay real estate taxes, the county "sells" a tax lien against the property.

The process works like this—

- the county needs monies which are collected in the form of taxes

- a property owner falls in arrears

- in an effort to collect its money, they county encourages investors to pay these taxes through a tax lien auction

- as an inducement, the investor can collect a high interest rate from the property owner when the tax is eventually paid. Interest can be as high as 25% every six months in Texas and up to 16% in Arizona. Maximums are set by the individual counties.

Tax liens are a little understood segment of investing that has usually been left to "experts". Today, this is no longer the case, as Counties are eager to get as many people involved in the auction process as possible. There are not enough investors for the number of tax liens available.

Why? Because investors run out of money before all tax liens are auctioned. Today, there are hundreds of thousands of available tax liens across the country and counties are eager for someone to step up to the plate and pay these taxes.

Due diligence is required to be successfully involved in tax liens auctions. Many of the unsold liens are useless parcels of land, some just narrow easements along the road; others are large parcels of land surrounded by desert with no access.

There are parcels with beautiful homes on which taxes were not paid due to oversight or lack of money.

The average tax due in developed parcels may be available as low as one and two thousand dollars and as high as tens of thousands of dollars.

Today, many home builders do not pay their taxes on undeveloped lots, knowing that even if someone does not purchase these tax liens, the developer will not loose his properties because the county does not want to be a landlord. The county knows that eventually, the home will be built and the taxes paid at settlement.

I recently purchased 52 such liens on vacant builder's lots for less than $2,000.00 and Alex, one of my grandkids purchased 4 parcels with homes on them for less than $3,500.00. He managed to get 16%, I only got 13%. Matt, my grandson in Texas, picked 7 builders lots for $220.00 and get this—25% every 6 months. Those lots will not have homes on them for at least 3 years and that means he will get about $750.00. Not bad a return for a small amount of money!

Eventually, if the taxes are not paid in the allotted redemption period, you can foreclose and acquire the property for your own use. Want quick money than sell the property way below market value. It might be worth $1,000,000, but it only cost you several thousand dollars in back taxes.

By the way, a redemption period is that period of time in which the owner can pay his back taxes. It can vary from 3 months to 5 years, depending on the county. The average is two to three years; meanwhile you getting a high return on your investment.

Why not purchase these tax liens and make a nice profit? You do not have to do anything. The country will repay your investment, plus the agreed upon interest when the taxes are finally paid.

Beats a CD every time because a tax lien is paid first; before any other creditors, including the mortgage company and with a much higher return.

Where do you get this information? That is part of the challenge and the reason many do not know about it.

You can search the web for tax liens and find several places that will provide you with information for a fee, or you can search for the county treasurer offices in the counties of the state in which you are interested. Go to a section titled "tax sales" or something similar and check out the information. It is free.

Sibling Partnerships

It may be possible, even desirable, to combine sibling funds, especially when they're younger, to make more sensible investments. Just make sure that the kids are involved and help make any decisions.

Especially if they're pre-teens, keep them informed on a regular basis, and if they invest in a stock have them look at a performance chart on a weekly basis. It's important to keep them involved and motivated. Again, in my mind, long term CD's don't cut the mustard. It's like watching paint dry.

An investment club among the siblings, as outlined in the previous chapter is also a viable option.

Family Companies

In some families, the dynamics of investment are already in place among the adults. The kids could be to involved as limited partners, or even be set up an LLC (Limited Liability Corporation) in which they can become involved in larger projects such as rental properties.

If you own rental properties, share that information with the kids, and if you're involved in the management of these properties get them involved. Share with them the pros and cons and let them experience firsthand the work involved and the results achieved with such an investment.

Small family companies are excellent teaching tools. Make sure your kids know about the company, what you do in it and, possibly, give them a small job.

My son Paul is a massage therapist who owns a Wellness Center. Rather than have a laundry wash the sheets used by the three therapists at the Center, he purchased a commercial washer and dryer and has his 14-year old son, Alex, do the laundry. Instead of paying a laundry company, he pays his son, who saves half of his income. His daughter, Maizie is thinking about developing a jewelry business where she'll use her creative talents to design inexpensive jewelry and ask people having garage sales to allow her to sell her designs. That's thinking out of the box!

Another son, Bob, has a multilevel market company selling nutritional supplements. His two daughters, Jenna and Kristin, are involved in the venture and sell organic cosmetics. Matthew isn't into selling cosmetics, so he's not participating in this opportunity.

Louise, the mother of James and Justin, is in real estate and has no potential jobs for her kids, but they certainly are aware of real estate. They were my partners-in-training on my first manufactured home project.

Diane is a photojournalist and not married. She has no kids, but is teaching Alex, her nephew, about photography, because that is one of his interests.

Even though a family business sounds exciting and is a source of income for the family, I don't suggest that your grandchild invest funds in a family business.

How would you determine your return on investment? How

would you sell your stock? How do you get your money back? It might prove to be an uncomfortable situation, so it's best not to create it in the first place.

A family business is a great place to learn, but not the wisest place to invest, especially for a youngster.

Outside Investment Clubs

Another thing you might consider is a local investment club. People, usually adults, gather on a regular basis to discuss their investments. These groups might also pool their money and invest as a group.

Members are responsible for presenting ideas to the club, which means they have to do research. This is just the type of exposure a youngster needs.

Why not find one of these clubs, or even start your own within the family or among your friends?

Whatever you do, you'll have to guide and encourage your grandchildren. They'll get sidetracked with school, sports, friends, extracurricular activities, etc. You have to make suggestions for areas of research on the Internet, encourage their every-changing dreams, and, most importantly, ask for their opinions on these various questions.

I like taking my grandchildren (not all at the same time!) to a book store with a coffee shop where, over hot chocolate and coffee, we discuss their plans and investments. Books on any subject are available right there if we want to pursue a new line of thinking.

Whenever I ask them if they want to go to the book store, they already know the purpose and are always willing and eager to go. They know there will be interesting conversation, some hot chocolate or a smoothie and, when pressed, Pop-Pop will buy them a book. I find Sunday afternoon or early evening the best for these get togethers.

Investors should think of their investments in terms of ownership. You do not own a stock or a piece of paper, but a piece of the company.

Roth IRA's

I also suggest that you inform your grandkids about **Roth IRA's** and **Roth 401k** accounts. They will be responsible for their own financial security, so when they begin their working lives they need to automatically save in one of these two vehicles.

After income tax, money is placed into one of these two plans. Aside from helping provide retirement funds for the future, all gains from these monies are tax-free. Unlike a traditional IRA or

401k, all withdrawals are tax-free. I can't repeat that often enough. That will make a huge difference in what will be available to our grandkids in the future.

The only basic difference between the two plans is that the **Roth 401k** is employer sponsored, and the **Roth IRA** is a plan to which you contribute independently of the workplace.

I would also suggest that the **Roth IRA** be a self-directed plan, which would allow your grandkids to invest in real estate or even in their own business. Remember, properly executed, these tax-free plans can produce huge monetary results. Of course, when the time comes, your grandchildren will need to seek the guidance of a tax counselor and/or a tax attorney. But what's important is that they know, as they are entering the work force what their options are.

Sources of Funds

- Both sets of grandparents

- Parents

- Family members

- Odd jobs

- Small businesses

- Donated stock

Potential Investments

- Savings Accounts, Money Market Accounts

- Stocks

- Mutual Funds

- Real Estate

    - REITS

    - Local Real Estate Investment Companies

    - Tax Liens

Funds for investing can be commingled with siblings funds, for greater leverage.

CHAPTER FOURTEEN

Is Math Important?

You bet it is! If you don't know your math, you'll end up taking a bath.

It's very important to understand that our grandkids will have a difficult time surviving financially unless they understand basic math. Algebra and calculus are very important if you want have a future with jobs in the new innovation age, but still everyone needs to understand of basic math.

Yes, I'm talking about 5th grade math. I'm talking about having an idea of what a simple answer would be to a simple problem such as knowing what your change should be after a cash transaction, or knowing when a discount is not a discount.

Many people make bad decisions because they don't understand simple math. Our grandkids need to understand the need for being competent in simple math, regardless of their chosen careers.

In a Wall Street Journal.com article, Jonathon Clements states that the saving rate remains close to zero, consumer debt is up over

7% and the Pew Research Center reported that half of Americans rate their personal finances as fair or poor.

Financial reckless is not the total answer. Lousy math skills are a major culprit. Many do not understand compound interest. Compound interest is good when we earn money on our investments, it's bad when we pay finance charges on our finance charges from reckless credit card use.

People do not understand and often miscalculate the savings of compound interest, on interest saved by paying extra on our mortgages, our credit cards and other debt.

Retailers recognize that the American public is weak in math and they take advantage of that in their pricing structures.

For example, which is a better buy? You see a $125 item that is discount 50% and therefore $62.50 at the register. Another store has the same item, priced at $125 discounted 20% at the rack plus another 30% at the register. Most consumers would simple add the two discounts together and assume that they will be getting a 50% when they purchase the item. The sale price would be the same in both stores.

Not so. In the second store, the 20% discount would equal to $25 making the item $100.00 at the rack. At the register it will be discounted another 30% for an additional discount of $30. The final sale price would be $70 rather than the $62.50 price at the first store. That's $7.50 out of your pocket.

Also, recognize that items are priced ending in odd pennies

because that makes it harder for most people to mentally calculate prices.

When you're in a restaurant, you should have an idea of how large the tab should be before you get the bill. That means, you need to be able to mentally calculate the cost of the items ordered. The way to do it is round up the costs of the items to the nearest dollar and add them up mentally. If the total bill is higher than expected, you will know to check it out for errors.

That goes for tipping. It helps to be able to calculate a 15% or 20% tip in your head.

The same goes for mentally knowing how much a commission on a stock trade will cost you, how much a mutual fund charge will cost you, how much that broker's commission really affects your wallet, how much is that 15% or 20% you'll need to put down to get a better interest rate on the home you want to purchase, how to calculate the true mileage you're getting on your car, quickly calculate your cash-on-cash returns on your investment. The list is endless.

Sometimes you learn the hard way, as I did.

Way back in the late 1950's, one of my first jobs was driving a bakery truck, delivering bread, rolls, donuts and pastry to local corner grocery stores. Super markets were just beginning to show their heads.

In the bakery industry, all product delivered to the grocer was on consignment. The driver was responsible for finding and constantly monitoring the fine balance of what could sell on any given day. Anything that was delivered and not sold was then returned to the driver at the end of the week, when the grocer paid his bill.

The driver was responsible for creating the bill predicated on deliveries during the week and the bakery presented the driver with a bill for the amount of product taken from the plant. Part of the formula for creating the monies owed the plant was a 7% allowance for product not sold. In other words, the driver had a 7% cushion. If he took more than 7% as returns from the grocer, it came out of his pocket.

The difference between what the driver collected from his accounts and the payment of the bakery bill was the driver's to keep. That small amount of extra cash acted as an incentive because it was treated as cash and therefore unaccounted for and didn't show up as taxable income.

It took me very little time to realize that I wasn't making the money that I should have. Something was wrong and I couldn't put my finger on the cause. I eventually spoke to one of the older deliverymen and he immediately told me what the problem was. Returns—either I was leaving too much product, resulting in taking back more than the 7% allowance, or the grocer was cheating me.

I began to fine tune my deliveries, but I soon discovered that the problem was that I didn't know how to count.

Some of you might be old enough to remember going to the

grocery store where there were no cash registers and no adding machines, much less scanners. The grocer itemized and totaled your bill on the brown paper sack. Those guys were good at math and very fast. That didn't mean they were all honest. They were fast and all errors were in their favor.

If the customer took notice at home of an error in the math, they would return the bag, point out the math error to the grocer who would say, "Sorry about that" and give credit on the next purchase.

Grocers were busy people. They knew when the bread man was coming and they had the "returns" ready for pickup, the credit due already figured out, as well as the bill. I would just verify that the amount of goods being returned was as stated. I never checked the math.

My point is that I had no concept of what 7% of the bill should have been, nor did I have a mental understanding of what the final bill should be. Because of that mental lapse, I was shortchanged by some grocers.

It was a costly lesson, though I'm glad to have learned it early in life.

It's not likely that your grandchild will be delivering bread, however, the lessons of understanding basic math still apply in today's world.

We used to call it being Street Smart.

CHAPTER FIFTEEN

What You Can Do to Stay Ahead of the Kids

All of us have different levels of understanding and varying comfort levels about money and finances.

My most important piece of advice would be to develop and maintain an open mind, recognizing ideas that will push your boundaries of comfort. We all have our limitations and our unseen boundaries. Most of the time, we don't realize what our comfort level is until we're confronted with an idea that doesn't fit into our thinking pattern or our mode of behavior.

Let Me Share a Story With You

I have four rental properties I purchased before the big run-up in prices in the mid-2000. I eventually stopped buying properties for rental purposes because I couldn't find one that would provide me with a positive cash flow. In other words, even with a conventional 20% down payment, my mortgage payment, taxes, insurance and emergency fund would be larger than the rent I could reasonably expect.

Prices kept rising and I watched my four rentals increase in value. Several months ago, (mid-2007), with the sub-prime scare, foreclosures and dropping prices, I decided to go looking again. I looked at hundreds of properties for sale, but none would give me a satisfactory positive cash flow. Housing was still expensive, and affordable housing wasn't available, unless you wanted to purchase a small condo.

Without going into boring details, let me tell you that I suddenly changed my paradigm and discovered manufactured homes. In my mind, manufactured homes (also called trailers or mobile homes) were not desirable. They were usually above ground, with the space beneath used for storage, and were usually found in lower income and rural areas, where there were no builders, no zoning, or in mobile home parks.

However, I found that the manufactured home scene was rapidly changing and my assumptions were no longer valid. Yes, there were still mobile home parks with old structures and rural areas populated with mobile homes.

But I realized that those manufactured homes were the last affordable housing available. I had never thought of these types of homes as an investment. In fact, I was somewhat astonished that I suddenly found myself thinking about making money on something that I previously had considered undesirable.

I started to investigate, and the more I learned, the more I wondered why other investors weren't seeing what I was seeing.

I was seeing affordable housing. I was seeing an opportunity. The reason investors and mortgage and title companies shy away from manufactured homes is because of misconceptions and old invalid ideas.

With further investigation, much legwork and many telephone calls, I put together a team specializing in the construction, setup, and financing of these manufactured homes. I've even found financing for all potential buyers. These homes don't look like manufactured homes when my team is finished. They look like any standard home, but they sell for up to 30% less than similar homes in the neighborhood. All I do now is look for suitable locations for these manufactured homes, and I make tens of thousands of dollars per home. This year I expect to do eight such projects.

Where do I find the opportunities? Well, to tell you the truth, they're coming my way from others. The mortgage broker liked what I had put together and told me of other possible opportunities. The dealer I purchased my first manufactured home from was surprised at what I had put together (and he's in the business!) and steered me to a very profitable opportunity at the other end of the state. I wouldn't have been aware of this opportunity had I not changed my awareness.

A little out-of-the-box thinking and observation found me another source of income. I basically took different pieces of information and put them together to form a viable opportunity for myself.

Basically, you'll have to overcome habits and inertia. You can't expect different results if you keep doing the same thing over and over again. I believe that's called insanity.

I love attending those seminars that promise me quick riches, and I watch the TV programs that do the same. I seldom buy anything, but I search for ideas. Ideas are free and the investigation of those ideas that intrigue me is also free for the most part. I go to my favorite book store or library and check out books on the subject. I might end up buying one or two, but then, that's the inexpensive cost of my education.

A website you might find beneficial to educate yourself on trading and the stock market is www.StockTradingTechniques. com. It is a free site dedicated to educating investors to be profitable stock traders.

So, to help your kids, your grandkids and even yourself, do the same things you would expect them to do in order to accumulate the cash you've promised.

Remember, this project is a two-way street. You lead the kids as they push you into unexplored territory.

Sources of Information

A. There are *Rich Dad* and other valuable books available for adults.

B. The book stores are full of books on wealth, finances, investments, real estate and making money.

C. The Internet.

D. Free seminars.

E. And most important—

DO SOMETHING AND DO IT NOW—ACT!

Although it's never too late,
don't procrastinate any longer!

CHAPTER SIXTEEN

The Importance of Goals

Everything you just read will only work if you set goals and teach your grandkids to set goals. The ability to set and achieve goals is essential to success in any endeavor.

You, as well as your grandchildren, need to set a goal to pursue the idea—and it is only an idea at this point in time. Then the idea of financial independence becomes a reality.

Setting goals puts you in charge of your life.

Create a Vision

We spoke earlier of daydreaming. Daydreaming is the creative aspect of establishing a vision; it is the seed that will grow into reality if acted upon.

As kids, we were taught to stop wasting time daydreaming, and yet that's the catalyst to creativity. Everything in existence that was created by man came from daydreaming. Da Vinci was a daydreamer; Henry Ford was a daydreamer; everybody is a daydreamer.

The only difference is what one does with those daydreams. If acted upon, they will become reality.

Help your grandkids plan and shape their future. Ask them what they want to do, what they hope to become, how they want to spend their lives, and where they want to be in 15 or 20 years.

Do they want to be a ball player, an engineer, a ballet dancer, a scientist, a business owner or a self employed professional? Talk to them about how they expect to get to that position in life. What schools should they attend? What part-time jobs they might take to see if that is what they like?

It's never too late to start. Help them create multiple visions. They're likely to change their minds numerous times, but that's to be expected as they search for their own identities and expand their interests.

Focus

Be clear in what you want to accomplish. Your goal is to help your grandkids reach financial independence. How you do that is subject to change and revision, as you proceed toward that goal.

Every grandchild is different and you'll need to focus on their uniqueness to help them move forward. It may not always be as quick and easy as you would hope, but focus. Focus on what you want to accomplish and why it's such an important goal.

And don't forget to pass on this piece of information on to our kids. They, too, will need to focus to reach their goals, no matter their age.

Write Down your Goals

A daydream needs to be nurtured to become a reality. Remember, you're acting as a mid-wife in this creation.

For an idea to become reality, it has be formed in the mind, visualized, vocalized and acted upon. Nothing else will work.

When you're developing a daydream, you're visualizing something, be it a number in a checking account, a new home, a trip to Africa or an elaborate dinner in previously unaffordable restaurant.

To make that something come true, to make it a reality, you have to act upon it. How bad you want that dream to come true will determine if and when it happens. If you procrastinate, it will never happen. If you write down steps that you'll take to make it happen, then you are on the way to making that daydream a reality.

Write down these goals and steps in the first person (I), and in the present tense ("I have" rather than "I had" or "I will"), as if you already have what you expect. Don't write "I want"; write as if it has already happened.

Keep these written goals handy and refer to them daily. Seeing them daily in writing will help to keep you focused.

Again, share this information with your grandchildren. They'll have to do the same to stay motivated.

Affirmations

To stay on track, you have to mentally repeat your goals and desires. This, in my opinion, is very important because it keeps that goal at the forefront.

What good is it to create the goal, write it down and forget about it? The thinking will spur the action. You'll find yourself doing the things that need to be done to realize the goal.

Goal-setting and the steps to achieving it is an active process that leads to tangible results. Every time you take a step that needs to be addressed in this process, you're that much closer to your goal.

It's very important that you relate this to your grandchildren. Although they subconsciously know that they have to act to get results, imparting this information to them now makes goal-setting a positive process, a process that is proactive rather then reactive.

So decide on your dreams and make a plan.

Setting goals puts you in charge of your life.

CHAPTER SEVENTEEN

The Only Reason Why This Program Might Not Work!

There's no magic in doing what I suggest, but it does require some effort, both on your part and your grandchild's part. This is no get-rich-quick scheme such as chain letters, make a million bucks in two week offers, letters from Nigeria offering you a shot at imaginary cash, get rich in real estate next week through foreclosures, buy property without any cash, get the secrets of inside traders, etc., etc., etc., well, you get the picture. There are no legitimate get-rich-quick programs or fast avenues to wealth unless you inherit the money.

This project takes effort. How much effort? Well, that depends on you. The biggest reason this might not work is procrastination.

There are a lot of excuses to put this off. Some of them might be legitimate, but in the end they are still excuses.

When is it a perfect time to do something? The most common response is, "I don't have enough time". Well, you have the same amount of time as Mother Teresa, Stephen Hawking, Nicolas Copernicus, Stephen King, Albert Einstein, Dick Tracy, Jane Doe and everyone else.

From the Investors Business Daily

Successful people have mastered the following –

- How you think is everything. Always be positive and think success not failure.

- Avoid a negative environment.

- Decide upon your dreams and goals. Write down specific goals; develop a plan to reach them.

- Take action. Goals are nothing without action.

- Don't be afraid.

- Just do it.

- Never stop learning. Go back to school, read books, acquire new skills and keep an open mind.

- Be persistent and work hard. Success is a marathon not a sprint. Never give up.

- Learn to analyze details. Get all the facts, all the input and learn from your mistakes.

- Focus your time and money. Don't let other people or things distract you.

- Be innovative; be different.

- Deal and communicate with people effectively. Learn to understand and motivate others.

- Be honest, dependable and take responsibility, otherwise the other suggestions won't matter.

Another reason might be, "I don't have enough information or knowledge". No successful person had enough knowledge at some point in their lives prior to becoming successful, but they had determination and drive. They set a goal and set out to achieve it.

How about, "I don't have enough money?" That's always a good excuse, but that shouldn't stop you from getting the project going. Involve other family members, combine assets. Start small, but start. Find a way!

As I mentioned earlier, I asked two of my long time tenants what they would do if they suddenly found themselves with $5,000. Both mentioned that they would spend the money, rather than pay down debt or invest. That mind set will keep them as my tenants for a long time.

The stakes are huge because times are changing, but most folks will just exist from day to day, not being too concerned about either their future or the future of their grandchildren. The subconscious I-won't-think-about-it-syndrome.

And don't tell me they have to learn the way you learned—the hard way. No one showed you and you did okay. That might be true, but wouldn't you have appreciated some quality guidance along the way?

That reminds me of another story. I have a handyman who does small jobs for me at my rentals. He lives with his girlfriend in a rental, though not one of mine. They're both about 50 years old. Jim (not his real name) is always complaining about his landlord.

In any case, I was involved in a project (with two of my grandkids as partners in training) which would provide perfect housing for Jim. He and his girlfriend, Ann, could purchase this home, which was brand new and larger than what they had at the present, and in a better neighborhood, for only $150.00 more than the rent they were paying. In addition, the location was perfect for future appreciation.

I gave Jim the name and phone number of a mortgage broker that specializes in manufactured homes. This broker had always managed to find funds for FHA housing, and my project would be no different.

To make a long story short, I eventually found out that these people never called the broker to get qualified to purchase the house. I realized that they were procrastinating, afraid—of what I don't really know—but they put off calling the broker to get approved. They procrastinated for weeks. I finally called the broker in their presence. They gave their Social Security numbers to the agent and two days later they were approved for their loan.

They're now the proud owners of a dream house that will only appreciate because of its desirable location.

Don't procrastinate.

The best time to do something is now. Can't? Pick a date, find the time and find a way.

CHAPTER EIGHTEEN

Opportunity Is Always Knocking

O pportunity is always knocking, but you have to hear the knock and open the door.

I think this is another lesson you can teach your grandchildren on their way to becoming financially savvy.

I'm a firm believer that you create your own reality. You create your reality by taking your dreams, thoughts and desires and making them a fact, making them a reality.

I don't have to tell you that everything begins with a thought. Once you start talking about the thought, then acting on it, you make the thought come to fruition.

Yes, it takes effort, persistence and determination, but you and your grandkids, can do it. There may be, and in many cases will be, setbacks, but if that stopped folks who believed in what they wanted we would still be living in the Stone Age.

Throughout time, people have spotted opportunities and persued them. Others saw the same opportunities but dismissed them as impossible. Yet others never realized there was a knock on the door.

Teach your grandkids to be open-minded and receptive to new, sometimes strange, sometimes conflicting, ideas. They don't have to agree with them, or adopt them, but they should be aware of them.

The great gift is to be able to take divergent pieces of information and bring them together in a new idea to solve a problem or create an opportunity. That's what innovation is all about.

Did you ever realize that change always comes from without?

Fast food wasn't originally thought of by the restaurant business, but by a salesman of milk shake machines.

The operating system that most computers run on today wasn't developed by Microsoft, but was conceived by someone else. Bill Gates saw an opportunity and ran with it.

The cotton gin wasn't developed by cotton farmers, the automobile wasn't developed by buggy manufacturers and credit cards weren't developed by banks, but by oil companies to sell their gasoline.

These ideas and thousands of other ideas that transformed our lives were the result of realizing needs and turning them into solutions.

I was fortunate to recognize such an opportunity when I got involved in manufactured homes. Even though I recognized that manufactured homes produced affordable housing in our area, I found out that no one made that knowledge available to the people who needed the information. There was a disconnect between the manufacturer, the seller and the buyer or investor who needed a loan on a manufactured home.

Once I discovered that manufactured homes were sold and financed as automobiles, things began to fall into place and I was able to put together many deals with great ease. Something that would have been impossible for me, had I not taken several pieces of different information and brought them together into a new idea.

Sometimes you have to recognize an obstacle as an opportunity. A case in point was my getting Jim my handyman, to purchase one of my projects.

I knew that Jim needed extra space to keep his truck and trailer off the street. This particular property had a rear entrance to a large paved RV space in the back of the house. Perfect.

But, as you know, procrastination kept him and his friend Ann from making the decision to purchase. To me that was an obstacle to selling the house quickly. By making a phone call for Jim and Ann, I took the pressure off them to make that decision. Once they found out they qualified for a loan, they were like two kids in a candy store.

By having this information, I was able to sell my property before it was finished, get my money and move on. Jim and Ann were grateful for the reduction in the price of the house, which I was able to give them because I didn't have to pay a realtor.

A win-win situation for everyone.

You don't have to act on every opportunity, but you should learn to hear the knock. Sometimes the opportunity is seized by someone else, and you slap yourself on the forehead with "Why didn't I see that before?" Or, it bursts on the scene like a flash of lightning, a sudden realization of what might be. Usually it sneaks up on you, but you're too involved to see it.

Tell your grandchildren that they don't have to act on all these ideas and revelations, but they should be aware of what they are—opportunities.

Let's put that into another context—opportunity never knocks! It's waiting there for someone who has the knowledge and information to recognize it for what it is—an opportunity.

Opportunity knocks constantly and on many doors simultaneously.
It waits for someone who sees it for what is—an opportunity— and opens the door.

A List of Dos and One Do Not

- DO teach your grandkids to be critical and analytical thinkers.

- DO teach your grandkids to be aware that ads are designed to separate them from their money.

- DO teach your grandkids that "cool" is to be confident, to be a leader and not a follower.

- DO teach them to set goals.

- DO be supportive—and involved.

- DO be encouraging—and involved

- DO be a motivator.

- DO teach your grandkids to be decisive.

- DO be a part of their adventure.

- DO NOT be critical or judgmental of their decisions and by extension, of them.

CHAPTER TWENTY

The Results

By now, the results should be obvious. My grandkids will learn and will continue to learn lessons of self-esteem, critical thinking, gaining knowledge, creativity, problem-solving, recognizing and analyzing opportunities and, most of all become confident. They'll learn the lesson of trust, in that my wife and I will trust them to follow our wishes that they won't touch the money until the age of 35, and after that spend only the income generated in the current year. Leave the accumulated principal alone!

You don't have to do it the way I did it. You don't have to start with $5,000 if you choose not to. Start with less and, instead of buying them more gifts for their birthdays, graduations or holidays, give them cash in form of a check and ask them to put it into their investment account. Give them some stock to start with, or possibly involve them in some of your financial dealings. If you're a landlord, take them with you when an occasion presents itself.

If you already invest in property, take them when you do inspections. Prepare them by explaining why you're doing this, and they'll quickly become eager participants.

You can set different guidelines, different rules, but the most important thing is that you act.

In the end, your children and grandchildren will learn lessons not available in schools, lessons that will give them tools to achieve and control the quality of life they choose in an ever-changing world.

For you, it will become the most rewarding experience of your life.

> **There is always one moment in childhood when the door opens and lets the future in.**
>
> Deepak Chopra

Suggested Resources

Canton, James, *The Extreme Future: The Top Trends That will Shape the World for the Next 5, 10 and 20 Years.*

DaSilva, Michael, *KidsWealth: Raising Money Smart Kids.* Currently offered by KidsWealth (USA), Inc as an e-Book.

Gray, John, *How to Get What You Want and Want What You Have.*

Kiyosaki, Robert T., *Rich Dad Poor Dad.*

        Rich Dad's Cashflow Quadrant.

        Rich Dad's Rich Kid Smart Kid.

        Rich Dad's Retire Young Retire Rich.

Leeds, Peter, *Understanding Penny Stocks.*

Stanley, Thomas J., Danko, William D. , *The Millionaire Next Door.*

Toffler, Alvin & Heidi, *Revolutionary Wealth.*

Investors Business Daily is an excellent financial and educational newspaper. Available at better newsstands, it can be delivered. It's a national newspaper.

www.Investors.com is a site maintained by *Investors Business Daily* newspaper. This site presents the basic of stock market investment and is an excellent tool for research by your grandkids.

www.KidsWealth.com The KidsWealth website where parents and grandparents can learn more about and purchase the KidsWealth Money Kit and supporting activity books.

www.StockTradingTechniques.com is a free site dedicated to educating investors to be profitable stock traders. It covers charting, identifying buy and sell levels, picking profitable industry sectors, fundamental and technical analysis, economic conditions, strategies, swing trading (but not day trading, a generally losing proposition) and a plethora of other subjects pertaining to investing in stocks. Although the focus is on technical analysis, the site will also help long-term investors to make better buy and sell decisions.

www.TheMotleyFool.com for good, unbiased, solid and basic advice on investing.

www.RedDoorGroupInc.com—a site that will give you insight into getting an above average return on your money

www.RichDad.com is the gateway to getting the Cashflow® board game so vital to giving the kids hands-on experience in financial decision-making. You can also order the books online.

www.YoungInvestors.com is an exceptional interactive website to teach teens and preteens the basics of money and investment.

www.PennyStocks.com—for information on penny stocks.

And your county treasurer's office for tax lien and trust deed information.

We alone are responsible for our successes. Let teaching our grandchildren about financial independence be one of these successes.

Acknowledgments

Nothing happens in a vacuum and neither did this book. And for making it happen I have to acknowledge the subtle input of my grandkids, Jenna, Kristin, Matt, Alex, Maisie, James and Justin. They do not realize, at this moment in time anyhow, how much input they have had into the content of this book. I know that they were not aware when they were being "interviewed" and peppered with questions.

Once the concept of the book took hold, and I realized that there was a book in me that had to be written, the moments, ideas and adventures I shared with these kids became part of the story. Thank you, Guys.

In the book I speak of serendipity. It played a big part in the having the idea come to fruition. When I began to write, I wrote 16 pages and I thought that was it. I said everything I had to say. Sixteen pages do not comprise a book.

As I was pondering this dilemma, a catalogue from our local Community College came in the mail. In it was a 2 evening course being offered by Tom Bird of Sedona on How to Write and Get

Published. I didn't have to be hit on the head with a sledge hammer to realize that opportunity was knocking. I signed up for and took the course. With his suggestions, and contacts, the finer parts of this book got done. I would never have found Sharon Garner, who did the proof reading and editing, Manjari Henderson, who design the cover and Jamie Soloff who was responsible for the interior design if I hadn't taken the class. Thanks Tom.

I want to thank my friends, those who took the time to read the rough draft of the book, offer their insights and allow me to quote them. They didn't get paid a dime, and I owe them "big time". I'd like the idea of having reviews from a parents and grandparents perspective. So, to Adele and Dick Montgomery, Florence and John McLaughlin, Patti and Ed Smith, Tina and Jeff Slade, Lisa and Eric Alinder, Jamie Finner and Cindy McLachlan—thanks.

At one point, my wife, Lorraine thought that I had become an appendage to the computer. It seems that for six weeks, I spent more time pounding on the key board, mostly writing and sometimes playing Free Cell (to take a break of course), than I did on anything else. That's over and Lorraine, thanks. Thanks for the support, the proof reading, the comments and the caring. I love you.

And kudos to you, the reader. Thank you for recognizing the need to help educated our grandkids and deciding to do something about it.

I know you'll have as much fun as I've had, and am still having.

To Contact the Author

You may contact the author by emailing him at:

chris@MoneySmartGrandkids.com

or visit him at:

www.MoneySmartGrandkids.com

Or you can write him via the publisher at:

KCL Publishing LLC
P.O.Box 318
8711 E. Pinnacle peak Rd.
Scottsdale, AZ 85255
www.KCLPublishing.com

9 780981 457505